I want to
matter

**YOUR LIFE IS TOO SHORT
& TOO PRECIOUS
TO WASTE**

Kathie Lee Gifford

W PUBLISHING GROUP

AN IMPRINT OF THOMAS NELSON

Published in Nashville, Tennessee, by W Publishing Group, an imprint of Thomas Nelson.

Thomas Nelson titles may be purchased in bulk for educational, business, fundraising, or sales promotional use. For information, please email SpecialMarkets@ ThomasNelson.com.

Unless otherwise noted, Scripture quotations are taken from the Holy Bible, New International Version®, NIV®. Copyright © 1973, 1978, 1984, 2011 by Biblica, Inc.® Used by permission of Zondervan. All rights reserved worldwide. www.zondervan.com. The "NIV" and "New International Version" are trademarks registered in the United States Patent and Trademark Office by Biblica, Inc.®

Scripture quotations marked ESV are taken from the ESV® Bible (The Holy Bible, English Standard Version®). Copyright © 2001 by Crossway, a publishing ministry of Good News Publishers. Used by permission. All rights reserved.

Scripture quotations marked LEB are from the Lexham English Bible. Copyright 2012 Logos Bible Software. Lexham is a registered trademark of Logos Bible Software.

Scripture quotations marked RGT are from the Revised Geneva Translation. Copyright © 2019 by Five Talents Audio. All rights reserved.

Cover photo: Jeremy Cowart

Cover design: Jamie DeBruyn

Interior design: Kristen Sasamoto

ISBN 978-1-4003-3969-3 (TP)
ISBN 978-1-4003-3970-9 (eBook)
ISBN 978-1-4003-3971-6 (audio)

Library of Congress Control Number: 2020943243

ISBN 978-0-7852-3664-1

Printed in the United States of America

24 25 26 27 28 LBC 5 4 3 2 1

Introduction

I wrote the lyrics to a song titled "I Want to Matter." It is the inspiration for this book. We all just want to matter, right? We want to love our people well and be loved in return. We want to have made a difference before we're called home to be with our Savior. We want to have lived a full life and not have any regrets.

I want to matter,
To have meant something special to somebody else,
To have made a small difference simply being myself,
To believe this three-ringed circus
Has fulfilled some earthly purpose.

I want to matter
Before I am gone,
To have once been the shoulder that someone leaned on,
To have been the safe harbor in someone's sad storm,
To know someone was blessed because I was born.

I want to matter
As much as I'm able,
To be more than a faded face framed on some table.

For if I'm to be framed, I want it to be
In somebody's heart for eternity.

Though I'm fragile and foolish and flawed, I'm sincere.
I want someone to fondly remember me here.
More than being praised, more than being flattered,
I need to know without a doubt that somehow I have mattered.

And if I'm really honest,
I would like to write one song
That someone will be singing long after I am gone.

My hope is that you'll read an entry each day and the stories I share will resonate with you. I want you to relive the moments that shaped you into who you are today. I hope each day brings you joy and revives your ability to wonder. At the end of each entry, I've included reflection questions. You don't have to write anything down. These questions are for the internal conversation you'll have with yourself. By the end of the book, I hope that you'll recognize how much you truly do matter.

DAY 1
Keeping Moving Forward

I was born into a wonderful family with two parents who knew very early on that they had an unusual child in me. They always showed their love in spite of my uniqueness, encouraging my adventures, circuses, concerts, and plays in the backyard. They let me raid the family pantry to open a corner store on our street. They smiled as I started the children's newspaper for our neighborhood. I'm eternally grateful to God for my parents.

Certain moments in life can take on a rich significance in retrospect. Take, for instance, the time I was kicked out of the Brownies. No, I'm not kidding. I actually was kicked out of the Brownies. They insisted I turn my beanie in. All because I had bought into the Join the Brownies, See the World propaganda.

I arrived at the first meeting super excited, but all I could see was the back of the beanie on the girl in front of me—who had bought into the same propaganda.

It turns out talking about the world is not the same as seeing the world.

For the first time in my young life I felt duped, disappointed that what I'd been told was not actually true. So, I started my own Brownie troop at home, and the organization took umbrage and asked me to never show up again. (I think I remember my parents giggling, but I'm not sure.) That experience has stayed with me for decades.

Disappointment can do a number on you, but only if you let it. I'm not sure where I got the drive and determination to keep moving forward, even at the ripe old age of seven, but it likely had a lot to do with my dad and mom.

Can you think of a time disappointment inspired a renewed sense of determination? What happened?

How did the outcome change you?

DAY 2
Do the Work

Today, I find myself at a point in life where the labels that technically apply to me could actually define me, if I let them. I'm a widow and an empty nester. Please don't throw in senior citizen—I already know that too. I'm basically alone for the first time in my long life. That thought by itself could either terrify me or thrill me. I'm trying very hard to be thrilled. Growing older is not for the faint of heart, but I truly believe that this next season of my life has the potential to be the best season in a life that, to this point, has been jam-packed with amazing opportunities and great adventures.

So, what's next? After lunch, that is.

I don't know, and that's the point. I can make the rest of my life what I want it to be. I can fill it up with people and have a celebration, sit by the fire and write an oratorio, or sit alone and have a pathetic pity party. For the very first time, it's my choice to make.

Some of my dreams have taken years to come true—like *Scandalous*, the Broadway musical that took thirteen years and fourteen million dollars to create, only to close after three weeks. Nothing I have ever dreamed has been easy. Nothing. Show business is brutal and has left many a carcass on the red carpet. I don't intend to be one of them.

As Stephen Sondheim once said to me, "You did the work."

Yes, I did, and I'm still doing it.

There is joy in the struggle of hard work, and there is profound pleasure in the sweat of it. I may have twenty years left in this life, or I may have twenty minutes. But I'm going to drink this life to the dregs while I can. Because there's no expiration date on your dreams.

What dreams of yours have taken years to come true? What work did you have to do?

How did you feel once your dreams were accomplished? Did your accomplishments bring forth new dreams and aspirations to work toward?

DAY 3
First Love

*L*ove at first sight is a real thing. The love I fell into with Yancy Spencer would stay with me in a profound way for the rest of my life, but also his.

Our situation was complicated due to the geography between us. By the time I was a senior in high school, Yancy had already been a professional surfer for several years traveling all over the world. There were no cell phones then, so we rarely got to speak. It was a great surprise when one day he called me at my house in Maryland inviting me to visit him and his family after Christmas in Pensacola. We had talked about getting married after I graduated.

Certain moments sear themselves in your memory—this was one of them.

After Yancy picked me up at the airport, he took me across the beautiful bridge on the way to Gulf Breeze, where he lived. He stopped the car on the other side, looked at me with his beautiful blue eyes, and said, "I'm so happy you came, Kathryn." (He is the only person in my life who ever called me by my real name.) "Seeing you has made me realize how much I love Pamela."

What?

It turned out that he had met a woman in the months before, and as often happens when you are young and impetuous, he would marry her a few months later.

I remember going home to Maryland after that weekend and banging my head over and over again against a door. Stupid for sure. But certainly an expression of the pain and the hopelessness I felt at the time.

Several years later Yancy called to tell me the wonderful news that he had come to faith in Jesus at Rock Church in Virginia Beach and realized the mistake he had made in marrying so hastily. His wife ultimately left him, but by then I had married my first husband, so we had missed our window of opportunity to be together.

Yancy went on to marry a beautiful Christian woman named Lydia.

Many years later, Lydia and their gorgeous eighteen-year-old daughter, Abigail, came to the studio to watch *Live with Regis and Kathie Lee*. Abigail was a gifted singer, dancer, and actress who wanted to pursue a career in the arts.

While there, I called the head of casting at ABC, who just happened to have watched the show that morning.

"Send her over," she said to me. "I want to meet her."

That's how capricious this business is. One minute you're an unknown entity sitting in a television audience, a few hours later you're auditioning for *All My Children*, and nine months later you're accepting a *Soap Opera Digest* award for Outstanding Female Newcomer.

Abby lived at our house in Connecticut for the first six months after her move to New York to work on the soap opera. We all adored her.

On the morning of February 14, 2011, Abby called to tell me that Yancy had died while surfing in Malibu, California. He'd had a heart attack. He was sixty years old.

❧ ❧ ❧

Do you remember your first love?
What was their name?

Did you stay in contact with your first love?
What special memories did you share?

A New World

I had a legal relationship with Paul Johnson, a brilliant composer, from April 23, 1976, to spring of 1983. Though Paul and I were married, we shared only one thing—our faith.

Back then divorce had much more of a stigma, and no one in my family was divorced. I believed that God could heal our marriage and prayed every day that He would.

Within a year of our wedding day I moved into our guest room and stayed there until our marriage was over. During those years I experienced the deepest loneliness of my life. I felt disgraced, rejected, and worst of all, like a failure at something I had hoped to be—a loving wife.

We put on a good, faithful face for the world we lived in, the contemporary-Christian music world, which was growing wildly in the '70s in California. But in private we were both desperately unhappy.

At one point we attempted counseling. We met with James Dobson, the founder of Focus on the Family, but it was a disaster. Dr. Dobson believed that I was the problem and that I should give up my career to attend to Paul's ambition and talent and keep his home neat and organized. Paul immediately responded, "No way! I don't want her waiting around at home for me. I *want* her to work." We sat in silence during the two-hour road trip home, no closer to any sort of breakthrough in our marital issues.

Though we had shared the same bed, we had never been truly intimate, and now we'd stopped talking too.

One day I came home from a three-week run on the road with Bill Cosby—a two-year stint where I was his opening musical act on his tour as a comedian. The lock on our front door had broken just prior to my leaving on the trip, and apparently Paul hadn't fixed it as he said he would because when I tried to go in the house, the door simply flew open.

I walked into our living room and found it completely trashed. My first thought was, *Oh my God, we've been robbed!* Then I noticed that the piano was missing, and it dawned on me, *No, he's left me.*

Today I remember this as one of the most deeply important moments in my life, when God met me at the point of my brokenness and said, "It's okay, Kathie. We can fix this. He didn't love you, but I do."

Tears streamed down my face all that day, but they were cleansing tears. I fell asleep in the guest room where I'd slept for years. I didn't miss him at all. There wasn't anything to miss. We both knew it was a whole new world now.

Why do you think we're so afraid of what
other people will think of us that we're
willing to sacrifice our happiness?

Have you experienced a moment of God's reassuring
love and commitment? What happened?

DAY 5
Closure

$\mathcal{S}$ ometimes opening up to the truth of a situation isn't as much about setting the record straight as it is about setting yourself straight in light of that truth.

I was living in New York City when my divorce became final.

I saw Paul Johnson just one more time. In 2011 my musical, *Saving Aimee*, which was ultimately named *Scandalous* when we got to Broadway, was having a run in Seattle, Paul's hometown. The morning of our two closing performances, my sister, Michie, called to tell me that Paul had bought a ticket to the matinee and wanted to know if he could say hello. Paul had stayed in touch with my sister Michie over the years. His father, who was an abdominal surgeon, had once saved her life, so it wasn't unusual for them to occasionally communicate.

Seeing Paul was the last thing in the world I needed or wanted that day. I was exhausted. But I had forgiven Paul years before and had prayed often for him since our marriage ended, so I called him and invited him to join me for lunch. He attended the matinee, loved the show, and asked if he could see it again that night. Afterward he joined me again, this time for dinner. He never said a word about why he left me the way he did or why he married me in the first place, and I didn't ask. I hugged him good night and wished him a happy life.

I still do.

Ironically, soon after I moved to the Nashville area, I was leaving Mojo's Tacos when a man who was with his wife stopped me and said, "Hi, I just want you to know that your first husband saved our marriage." His wife nodded in agreement.

I said, "I'm sorry, what?"

"Yes, we were on the verge of divorce and we went to see him. You know he's a marriage and relationship counselor now, right?"

I said, "No, I didn't know that, but I'm so happy he could save your marriage. He sure couldn't save ours!"

You've got to love God's sense of humor.

Has someone in your past surprised you
with the way they carried on with their
life? How does it make you feel?

Have you forgiven someone who you thought
you didn't have the power to forgive? How has
forgiveness made you a stronger person?

Treat Others the Way You Want to Be Treated

*R*edemption is available for everyone but is only effective
when it's embraced.

I was in Jupiter, Florida, scheduled to be a guest on the
popular *Dinah Shore Show*. The producers had also booked
the composer Paul Williams, actors Lee Majors and James
Brolin, and the Gatlin Brothers—Larry, Rudy, and Steve—for
the whole week.

The idea was to have Dinah surrounded by men who adored her, and they all did. She was America's sweetheart at the time. The problem was that Dinah's longtime manager, the legendary Henry Jaffe, had not signed another client in decades, until he signed me. And he had booked me to come on the show and announce that I was the new face of Diet Coke. My parents and the executives from Coca-Cola flew in.

I was excited as I stood in the wings, all wired up and ready to make my entrance near the end of the first show. But Dinah never announced me. She completely ignored the producers, the director, and the stage manager frantically signaling for her to do so.

The show ended, and I stood there, stunned. What could have happened? Was it just a technical mistake? My manager assured me that the next day's show would be different. Dinah had been confused—this time it would all go as planned.

But it didn't. The exact same thing happened, and I was completely mortified.

Finally, the producers assured me that they had convinced Dinah she couldn't do this again. She agreed to introduce me on the third day of shooting. I couldn't stay in my hotel room and feel sorry for myself. My family was there, and all the execs from Coca-Cola had agreed to stay as well.

That night we went to a local restaurant for dinner, and when my parents and I arrived, every diner in the place stood up and started applauding. I realized my audience was the staff and crew of *The Dinah Shore Show*. They wanted to offer their support after my three days of embarrassment.

I had dealt with the cruelty of what Dinah did in ignoring, even snubbing, me on her show and pretended I was just fine with all the delays. But, ironically, the kindness of these wonderful people who had watched it happen sent me flying into the ladies' room to sob my eyes out. I was grateful for each and every one of them.

The next day the show went off without a hitch. Dinah introduced me with her sugary Southern drawl. I sang a Barry Manilow song and sat down with the other guests for the interview. Dinah made all kinds of lovely, flattering compliments and maintained a fake smile.

Soon enough it was over. I made a mental note that no matter what happened—no matter how successful I would be blessed to become—I would never treat another person so disrespectfully or cruelly.

Has anyone purposely snubbed you and caused you embarrassment that you'll remember for a lifetime? How did you handle their disrespect?

Have you intervened, like the staff and crew of *The Dinah Shore Show*, to support someone who was being treated unfairly? If you did, how did your actions help that person?

I had met my friends the Gatlin Brothers in Nashville on the set of *Hee Haw Honeys*. Years later, we were in Florida for a taping of *The Dinah Shore Show*, so Larry Gatlin and I agreed to spend some time together. When it was time to meet up, Larry didn't come, so I asked his brother Rudy, "Where's Larry?"

Rudy looked at me nervously and said, "Uh, he must still be up in the room. Why don't you go check on him?"

"All right," I said. "What's the room number?"

Rudy told me, and I went up the elevator in search of the correct room. I knocked on the door and heard what sounded like Larry's voice.

"Wait a minute . . . let me get a towel," he said, kind of frantically. Suddenly the door flew open and there, indeed, was Larry wrapped in a towel, the darkened room behind him.

"Come on in, Kat," he said as he opened the door. He looked a mess. I was thinking something wasn't quite right, but surely he would find the light switch at any moment, get cleaned up, and go downstairs with me to join our group.

Instead he began talking feverishly. "Got to get to my

plane . . . they've got the engines running, gotta get to my . . . gotta get . . ."

"Get what, Larry? What's wrong?" I said, noticing now that he was sweating profusely and shaking badly.

I knew nothing about drugs. *Nothing.* But it was obvious that Larry was on way too much of something, and I had no idea how to help him.

"Larry, what can I do?" I asked, somewhat desperately. "Should I call someone to come?"

"No, no, no," he insisted. "Let me just get in bed for a little while and calm down. I'll be fine. Let me lay down for a minute."

"Okay," I said and continued to stand there, concerned and confused.

His shaking became uncontrollable, and he was clearly scared. "Kat, please hold me. Please, Kat, I can't stop shaking."

I did not hesitate. I got on the bed with my friend and held him as he cried, whimpered, shook, and sweated until the sheets were wet.

Finally—I have no idea how many hours later—he fell asleep in my arms like a baby. I waited until I was sure he was okay, then stood up. I looked back at him sleeping peacefully.

"Oh, dear Jesus," I prayed, "please help my friend."

I left quietly, closing the door behind me.

Soon afterward Larry went to rehab, where he got the help he so desperately needed. He's been sober for decades and has continued his incredibly successful career.

Larry never mentioned what had happened in Florida until one night at a Gatlin Brothers concert at Carnegie Hall in New York City. My husband Frank and I were seated in the mezzanine when Larry suddenly said, "Ladies and gentlemen, I want you to look over there." He pointed to me. "See her? See her? That lady is my dear friend, Kathie Lee Gifford. For the first time I want to thank her publicly for saving my life a long, long, long time ago. She saved me from getting on a plane and going to get more drugs that likely would've killed me."

I sat there, uneasy at the attention, but so happy for my friend.

"Stand up, Kathie," Frank said.

"No, honey." I just waved back at Larry and blew him a kiss. There was no need to stand. That's what friends are for.

Do you have a friend who has struggled with addiction? How have you supported them?

Friends are the family that you get to choose for yourself. Has a friend saved your life or impacted your future in a big way?

Never Lose Faith

*I*t's hard to tell this story. My sister Michie experienced undiagnosed horrendous gastric and intestinal problems after giving birth to her daughter. After collapsing at a church service, she was diagnosed with acute ulcerative colitis. Hopelessness was the prevailing prognosis. She was seriously close to death, and I could barely look at her or her precious baby, who I feared would never know her amazing mother.

My mother and Michie's husband, Craig, flew in from Maryland. The doctors discovered that 80 percent of Michie's five-foot-long large intestine was destroyed, leaving 20 percent that had the consistency of wet tissue paper. It had to be removed and an ostomy bag had to be attached to her small intestine.

To our amazement, Michie survived the operation. In the middle of the night, the hospital called to tell us: Michie had had a grand mal seizure and was barely holding on to life. She needed her mother and her husband, and she needed her sister to stay home and take care of her only child.

The hours agonizingly blurred one into another. Michie went on to have two more grand mal seizures. The doctor told Craig that it was time to say goodbye. He cried into our mother's arms, wailing, "God, Joanie, they've done such a number on her."

Then Michie fell into a coma, a coma none of us ever believed she would come out of.

Mom and Craig and I prayed. What else could we do?

All we could do was wait. I went to see Michie in her room and sat down next to her bedside. I was furious with God. How could He allow such a thing to happen to this unbelievably faithful person?

It was during this time that Michie suddenly emerged from the coma. She looked at me and said, "Don't curse God for this bag, Kathie. It means I get to live the rest of my life."

As overjoyed as I was that she had survived the surgery and all the seizures, I was devastated that I had lost all faith that God could heal her. It took several years after returning to Maryland for Michie to recover. But she did. And then she began to share her amazing experience of God's grace with others.

✿✿✿

Has your faith been tested? What happened, and how was your faith reinstated?

Have you experienced God's grace? How did His grace change your life?

Gentle Grace

One year after my niece Shannie was born we were told that she had pulmonary stenosis—a heart defect that would have to be watched closely as the days went by. A year later, after no problems in her health, Shannie went in for her regular checkup, and her doctors told her parents that she needed emergency surgery.

Shannie turned two years old at the Children's Hospital in Washington, DC. We had a little party for her with the other precious children who were suffering from all manner of diseases. It broke my heart to see that so many of them were alone, with no one to suffer with them. They were wards of the state. Shannie was scheduled for surgery the day of her celebration.

"Juice, Mommy!" she said over and over again that morning. "Hungry, Mommy!" She wasn't allowed to eat or drink anything, and her surgery kept getting delayed. We did our best to divert her attention.

"Let's walk down the hall, Shannie Roo," I suggested, using the nickname I loved to call her. Shannie, as tiny as you can imagine a two-year-old could be, was prepped for surgery and wearing her miniature surgical gown. One of the indelible pictures seared into my mind is the image of her walking down the hall with her little bottom peeking out at me, dragging her carved turtle by a string. She had no idea what pain awaited her. No idea what trauma was about to be put on her beautiful baby body. No idea that she might have celebrated her last birthday.

Shannie was eventually put onto an adult gurney that was to be taken into surgery. Only Michie and Craig were allowed to accompany her to the elevator where they could kiss their beloved child goodbye. When the elevator doors closed, Michie watched her "I've got this" husband sob like a baby.

But here's the reality: the day Shannie survived her surgery, two of the children in her wing died. We cried both tears of joy and tears of sorrow.

> Tender Savior, gracious Lord
> How can I express
> My grateful heart for all You do
> How You love, how You lead, how You bless
> Gentle Savior, loving Lord
> How can I repay
> The debt I owe for all You've done
> Every moment, every hour, every day
> Gentle
> Gentle grace, gentle grace.
> —"Gentle Grace" by Kathie Lee Gifford

Life is never so hard as on days like that when some are blessed to keep the one they love and others have to let a loved one go, and none of it makes any human sense.

How has grace impacted your life? How do you extend grace to others?

Hardships and loss do not make sense. When you face a challenging time, what do you do to move forward without losing your faith?

DAY 10

Our Convictions

*M*ichie was determined that God wanted her to tell her story of His faithfulness to her and her baby girl.

You see, there was a prevailing teaching at the time that sin caused all suffering and that God couldn't work miracles without first a confession of sin.

None of this is biblically true. Michie and I were booked

to appear on the *Praise the Lord* telecast. I told the producers that Michie and I would only appear on the show if we were allowed to sing three songs and allotted enough time for Michie to tell her testimony: that no, God didn't heal her instantly of her disease and no, He didn't heal Shannie instantly either, but He got them through both seasons of despair and never left their sides. He healed them through prayers and doctors and medicine. And that, too, was a miracle!

The telecast began with no mention of Michie or me as guests. It went on and on until it was almost time to wrap. Finally, I couldn't stand it any longer. I went to the senior producer to express my frustration only to be told, "I'm sorry, but the Holy Spirit is moving."

I exploded, "Well, the Holy Spirit is moving me to leave this place right now if you don't honor the commitment you made to my sister!"

The senior producer looked at me, terrified. No one was used to this kind of reaction from me, but I didn't care. I knew Tammy Faye was insecure and jealous of every other woman and hated to give up the spotlight, even for a second. I'd also heard she was having marital problems. I was truly sorry for her, but you don't let those truths overwhelm the truth that you have made a promise. God expects you to keep promises just as He does.

We finally were called onstage and sang one song, but Michie never did get the chance to share her testimony. As the final seconds of the telecast were winding down, Tammy Faye pretended to care about my sister and her daughter, but when the light on the camera went from green to red, she walked away from her midsentence.

Something huge in me died that day. I determined I would never again take one penny for any kingdom work. Never. And I haven't.

Only later I would learn that we had been in Charlotte on the very same day Jim Bakker admittedly had sex with a twenty-one-year-old girl named Jessica Hahn. Compassion washed all over me for Tammy Faye and for Jessica Hahn. I could relate to both women for different reasons.

When it comes down to it, our convictions are about all we have. They determine who we are. On the other hand, we can't control anyone else, but we don't have to hang with them.

Convictions are attitudes that are treated more like aspects of the self—they're not *just* opinions. What convictions define who you are?

Has anyone ever inserted their opinion about your conviction(s)? How did you react? Did their concerns impact you?

Never Settle

S oon after I moved to NYC in June 1982, I happened to be walking up West End Avenue when I noticed a familiar figure walking down the street toward me. We recognized each other at the exact same moment and said an awkward hello. It was Regis Philbin. Hardly an auspicious meeting. But "little is much when God is in it."

Three years later it was announced that Regis's cohost on *The Morning Show*, Ann Abernathy, was leaving the program to get married. I immediately called my agent, Sam, to tell him I wanted the job. I was restless and unfulfilled working at *Good Morning America*. Back then everything was on teleprompter and talent was encouraged not to "vary from the script." As an entertainer, I had grown weary of having so little creative freedom.

Somehow it got into the newspapers that I was considering leaving *GMA* to join Regis. I happened to be having lunch one day at Le Cirque restaurant in Midtown when I suddenly noticed the queen of the TV world, Barbara Walters, holding court at a table across the room. I waved obediently and she smiled and beckoned me with her index finger to come over to her table.

I was not close to Barbara or her inner circle, but I admired and respected her, and she had always been pleasant and encouraging to me. "What's this I hear about you joining Regis?" she asked.

"I don't know, Barbara. I want to, but everyone says I'm crazy. Why would I want to leave a major network morning show where I'm poised to get the number-one anchor job to join a local show in New York?"

Barbara didn't miss a beat. "Honey," she said with a chuckle, "Toledo is local."

I paused to consider her words. She continued, "If you and Regis click, you won't be local very long."

Of course, she was right.

I auditioned a couple of times and the sparks flew immediately. Soon after, ABC offered me the job.

I couldn't wait to get away from the teleprompter and start playing verbal gymnastics with the master of "television talk." Working with Regis was akin to playing ping-pong on a tightrope: dangerous and unpredictable but exhilarating. But I was still technically under contract with *GMA* on the first day of my new cohost gig on *The Morning Show*. I decided to use that technicality for a little comic relief. Just as *GMA* was going off the air at 8:58 A.M. I changed into big sneakers and raced down the street to make a breathless entrance after Regis had already begun at 9:00 A.M. He feigned annoyance at my tardiness and yelled, "Is this the way it's gonna be? Great." And we were off to the races.

There was no one like Regis then and there never will be again.

Life has taught me that if you want new beginnings, you must put in the work to create those sparks. You'll never be able to fly if you don't take the risks and at least try. Sometimes you must vary from the script so you can write your own.

Have you ever reached a crossroads where you had to bet on yourself so you could live out your dreams? What was the outcome?

Sometimes we need a friendly nudge so we can feel confident with our decision to go all in. Has anyone ever nudged you in the right direction? If so, what did they say to you? What made their push so powerful?

DAY 12
An Unexpected Miracle

*I*n the milestones of our lives we discover who we are. If we're blessed with the wisdom that comes with experience, we will also discover our purpose. And then our greater purpose.

Frank already had three grown children when I met him. He was also already a grandfather and certainly didn't want to go through the whole process again. Yet he thought it was completely unfair to deny me the gift of a child if it was something I truly wanted.

I had always loved children, but I was never one of those women who longed to be a mother more than anything else in life. By the time we were married I was thirty-three years old and starting to think my window of opportunity to have healthy babies was closing. I decided to let nature take its course and see where that led.

Honestly, I was so ecstatic to finally be in a loving, supportive, healthy, and sexy relationship that I truly wasn't longing for anything more. Three years after we got married, Frank and I went on a cruise along the Amalfi coast in Italy—one of our favorite places in the world. It was a perfect vacation in every way. One we had looked forward to before the start of the football season and the inevitable time that we would be apart while Frank covered the games.

No one was more surprised than I when, weeks after we returned home, I began to feel a little funny. Not sick, just different. Then something happened that had never happened to me before in my life. I sat before a picnic table full of fresh Maryland blue crabs and couldn't stomach the sight of them. They were and still are one of my favorite foods. I did some math. *When was my last period?* I couldn't remember at first until I realized it had been right before our cruise.

No . . . could it be? How could it be? I was astonished at the possibility after so much time.

We bought a pregnancy test at the drugstore and watched the little stick change to a resounding positive. I don't remember being thrilled, and I know for sure that Frank wasn't. But I did eventually rejoice, and so did he, knowing that God was going to bless us with a child.

This was not something we had prayed for, as so many couples do, but something that God had designed for a greater purpose than the fulfillment of our dreams. I had trusted that the Lord would bring it about if it was His will, and it obviously was.

Cody was born on March 22, 1990. He was eight pounds, fifteen ounces and delivered by emergency C-section. All babies are blessings, but for me, who had come to believe that I would probably never have a child of my own, he was also a miracle.

Have you received an unexpected
miracle that changed your life?

What blessings have you received that you never
asked for? How have those blessings impacted you?

Taking a Stand

*C*hanging the world doesn't have to be a large-scale thing—though sometimes small steps inspire major movements. You can impact your neighborhood, the school down the road, or where you work like no one else. There's always time to change the world, one child at a time.

In the early nineties, AIDS was a brand-new, terrifying, and largely misunderstood disease. Three months after Cody's birth, I attended a dedication on the Upper East Side of Manhattan of a new facility for newborn babies suffering from HIV or full-blown AIDS. I was deeply moved by the facility's courage when the rest of the world seemed to be paralyzed by fear of even getting close to these children.

On a hot June day on East Ninety-First Street, I held my very first AIDS baby. He weighed less than two pounds. In my other arm I held my eleven-pound healthy son. One baby born into suffering and pain, the other born into health, prosperity, and hope.

The injustice of that one moment forever changed me. All of the babies died. So, day after day, loving, caring volunteers came to the brownstone, now called the Cody House, to simply rock them—literally to love them to death.

That's why Frank and I decided to sue the state of New York to unblind HIV testing so at-risk women could be told their results and given the drugs needed to combat the possibility of their children being born infected with HIV or AIDS. We had learned that if these drugs were administered in utero, the chance of a child being infected went from about 25 percent to less than 8 percent. We had to change the law because although the results of the HIV testing had been tracked, they were not informing the pregnant mothers due to privacy issues.

We were still embroiled in this reality when we received an invitation from my friend Claudia Cohen to attend a dinner at her oceanfront home in East Hampton in 1995. Claudia was aware of our work with the Association to Benefit Children (ABC) and our ongoing lawsuit with the state of

New York, so she purposefully seated me next to New York governor George Pataki.

I took the next two hours to explain to the governor why we were suing the state.

He listened attentively and respectfully and, at the end of our basically one-way conversation, said three things I have never heard a politician say: (1) "I didn't know this," (2) "We're on the wrong side of this issue," and (3) "I'm going to do something about it."

Several months later Frank and I stood in the memorial garden of the Cody House and listened as Governor Pataki announced that all HIV testing was to be unblinded.

One year later the AIDS death rate went down in New York for the first time,[1] which can be attributed to the fact that the AIDS *birth* rate went down. One year later the unblinding of HIV testing was mandated in every state in the nation.

Has researching a topic changed your stance
on a controversial issue? How so?

What can you do to impact your neighborhood?
What steps do you need to take?

What More Can I Do?

*S*oon after our successful lawsuit to unblind HIV testing, Frank and I went to what we came to call "the world's most expensive lunch" with Gretchen Buchenholz. She had founded the advocacy organization ABC and was one of the advocates who fought for the lives of the innocent children dying because of HIV. We asked her a simple question: "What more can we do?"

She shared her plan to open a new facility to house the growing number of children who by then were benefiting from the newly discovered cocktail of drugs that, if administered during their mothers' pregnancies, would help them battle the disease. Frank and I pledged our help. We eventually purchased the Ronald McDonald House on East Eighty-Sixth Street. It had originally been part of an existing church.

For the next year and a half, we attempted to renovate it. But even when you're trying to do a good thing, you come up against all the bureaucracy of any large city that stands in your way. We were denied the permits we needed due to all of the building codes that restricted any possibility of renovation. We had no choice but to tear it down and build from scratch. So we did.

Our daughter, Cassidy, had been born on August 2, 1993, completing our family of four. Gretchen named the new building Cassidy's Place, and on October 24, 1996, we dedicated the four-story, state-of-the-art facility to house all of ABC and care for the growing number of babies living longer with the disease. Today, even as my children have married and begun their own families, the Cody House and Cassidy's Place are alive and well on the East Side of Manhattan.

Once you embark on the journey of changing your neighborhood, your heart yearns to do more. The gratification you'll receive from helping others is a memory that is forever stored in your heart. You'll never be the same, but that's the whole point.

How have you been changed by another
person's kindness and goodwill?

What memories of gratitude live in your heart
because of someone else's kindness and goodwill?

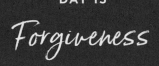

Forgiveness

I had been chosen to sing the national anthem at Super Bowl XXIX in Miami on January 29, 1995. ABC would be broadcasting, and Frank would be hosting the telecast live alongside Al Michaels and Dan Dierdorf.

"The Star-Spangled Banner" is one of the most difficult songs to pull off. Don't believe me? Just ask anyone who has performed it. Barry Manilow warned me to not look at the scoreboard because it would show me how many people were tuned in. So factor in the anxiety of, oh, say about a hundred million people watching you attempt it.

Terrifying.

It was time for last looks before heading off to the field to begin the game. With literally seconds to go, my makeup artist unwittingly stuck my left eye with the mascara wand, then my hairdresser, also unwittingly, sprayed hairspray into my right eye. I could not see more than a blur as I was led out before the biggest audience I would ever face.

Frank's voice reverberated all over the stadium.

"Now, to honor America, please join in the singing of our national anthem. . . . sung by television and recording star, my *wife*, Kathie Lee Gifford."

I couldn't believe he said that. I knew he was proud of me, but it was as if he were confirming to the whole world that the only reason I'd been chosen to sing was because I was sleeping with him. I wanted to kill him! But, of course, I couldn't because I would have had to find him first, and that was impossible since I was now *blind*. Then I heard the boos. They were coming from somewhere in the stadium, but I had no time to process this. The orchestra was playing the introduction.

"Oh, say can you see . . ." I began. "No, I can't!"

Gratefully the song came to a thrilling end as the jets flew overhead, the fireworks exploded, and the audience went crazy. There were no more boos, and somehow I was shuffled off the field and onto a plane to go home. I soon discovered that Howard Stern had asked his fans to boo me when I was introduced.

The whole experience was completely surreal, as so many moments in my life have been. At that time, I had never met Howard Stern and I never listened to his show.

Thirty years later, I was in my makeup room and heard he was in the studio to announce *America's Got Talent*. I felt the Lord clearly say to me, "Go down and say hello to Howard." So, I listened to the Lord and wished Howard the very best with the show. Later, he called me and apologized. He asked me for forgiveness. He said that I pissed him off because I was everything he wasn't.

I had already forgiven him thirty years ago. In my life,

I've learned that holding grudges doesn't do anyone justice. I've also come to believe that it inhibits the flow of blessings into your life. Forgiveness has given me feelings of understanding, empathy, and compassion for others. Forgiveness can also free you from someone else's control.

Have you forgiven someone who has wronged you?
How has forgiveness provided you with emotional freedom?

Is there someone in your life that you need
to forgive but have chosen not to? How can
you take steps to forgive this person?

DAY 16
False Narratives

In March 1996 a man stood up in Congress and accused me of operating sweatshops in Honduran factories to manufacture my Walmart clothing line. He represented himself as a human rights activist, when in reality, he worked for UNITE, a garment industry lobby that desperately wanted to unionize the world's largest retailer.

In six months we would be opening Cassidy's Place after spending several years of our lives building it and millions of our dollars paying for it—most of the money coming from my Walmart profits.

All hell broke loose. Nobody cared about the truth. I went to every network I had worked for—including my employer at the time, ABC. To their shame, and my disbelief, not one of them reported the truth about my accuser's lies, about me, or the truth about him. The vicious attacks went on for months with no sign of letting up. We turned off the TV and avoided grocery and convenience stores—everywhere and anywhere that the dreaded tabloids peddled their poison.

There were calls for me to be fired from *Live with Regis and Kathie Lee.* Thankfully ABC understood that the accusations were false and designed to ultimately damage Walmart's reputation with no regard to mine.

I was grateful for their support but still hurt when they refused to cover my accuser's apology to me and my family. During the darkest period of the insanity my longtime friend Larry King called to ask me to come on his show.

Larry asked me whether my sales had taken a hit in light of all these baseless accusations, and I told him that, actually, it was quite the opposite. They had gone through the roof.

I confirmed and proceeded to tell him how just the other day at my show a lady had stood up and gestured to the outfit she was wearing. I recognized it immediately as a dress from my Walmart collection.

"You look great," I told her.

She said, "When that man stood up in Congress and accused you like that, I got so mad I went straight to Walmart and bought five of your dresses!"

Finally, after diving in to fight *real* sweatshops, we got laws passed to protect against the abuses. The "hot goods" provision of the Fair Labor Standards Act, which had languished in Albany, New York, for nine years, was passed in nine days when Frank and I got involved. I spent a year commuting to Washington, DC, to sit with President Clinton to form an alliance between retailers and (real) human rights advocates. I testified before Congress, an audience I never dreamed I'd have (and didn't enjoy at all, trust me).

Some people still believed, in spite of all the evidence to the contrary, that I knowingly and willfully ran sweatshops. I finally had to accept that these people would never change their opinions because the false narrative somehow fit their agenda.

I am so grateful to all the people who continued to believe in me and continued to trust my heart through the most difficult times of my life.

Can you think of the people who stood by you during a difficult time in your life? Who were they?

How did their allegiance help you overcome the challenging events? Have you had an opportunity to stand by someone when they needed support?

DAY 17
A Revelatory Moment

On May 1, 1997, Frank met a woman at the Regency Hotel on Park Avenue in New York City and committed adultery. He had been set up to be caught by a revolting tabloid magazine.

I can't say it any more plainly, and even writing those words all this time later pains me.

For years I avoided driving down Park Avenue, hoping to avoid the natural emotions it would trigger.

I also began sessions with a trusted counselor. Frank immediately asked me to forgive him, and I did. I had to. My whole faith is built on the foundation of forgiveness: Jesus died for *me* for the forgiveness of *my* sins. We cannot withhold from others what He has freely given to us.

But I struggled with the casual way in which Frank expected us to get on with our lives—as if nothing had happened. I couldn't automatically feel the same way about him that I always had. He wasn't my hero anymore. When I shared this with my therapist one day, he said words that are now emblazoned on my heart:

"Kathie, if you can't forgive your husband, forgive your children's father."

It was a revelatory moment. It took my eyes off of me and set them squarely on my children, who were still completely unaware of their father's unfaithfulness. My children's father was a wonderful, loving, gentle, compassionate, generous, and sweet man. He was easy to forgive because I knew his heart.

Now, with new eyes to see, I prayed an almost impossible prayer. "Lord, please give me a deeper desire for Frank than I have ever had for him, even more than at the beginning."

This was an epic request. I was *crazy* in love with Frank then, and grateful to finally have the kind of exciting, thrilling, ecstatic love I'd only known about from books or movies.

To my surprise, God answered my prayer and gave me a desire for Frank unlike anything we had ever experienced. Every time we made love it was truly healing for me.

"Now I see how you're gonna get back at me, Kathie. You're gonna kill me," he loved to say.

The laughter returned, and our children grew up to be the most extraordinary two human beings I've ever known. By the time they learned the truth of what had happened, they knew an even deeper truth: their parents loved them and each other enough to trust in God's healing.

Our lives can take some unexpected twists and turns. Some come as the result of our choices; other times it's because of someone else's. No matter how hard things might become, it's never too late to bring beauty from the ashes. If you find yourself in such a place as I did—in the midst of a season of great difficulty—take a deep breath, prayerfully face the truth, find a Christian counselor to help you figure out your next steps, and trust God to lead you through.

What unexpected twists and turns have you experienced because of your own choices?
What role did forgiveness play?

What unexpected twists and turns have you experienced because of *someone else's* choices?
What role did forgiveness play?

Making My Own Music

*M*any years ago, so many I can't remember, I was singing a song into my father's movie camera. I stopped singing a cappella at one point and said, "Where's da moo-sic, Daddy?" I can still hear my daddy so tenderly respond, "Oh, honey, you have to learn to make your own music."

It has taken me a lifetime to learn to make my own music. For decades I sang and recorded hundreds of songs by brilliant composers—everyone from Joni Mitchell to the Bergmans, Sondheim, Hamlisch, and others, never dreaming that my father literally meant what he'd said. Sure, I'd written silly songs my whole life, little ditties and novelty songs. But, as is often the case, one day it all crystalized.

I had just closed on Broadway. I had been taking over for Carol Burnett for three months in a Sondheim "review" called *Putting It Together*—one of the most profound professional experiences of my lifetime. It was exhausting but thrilling.

Right before my debut, a stagehand strike was looming, and it looked like I might not get the chance to actually perform. I did my one and only run-through with the cast, costume, sound, and the orchestra, then went to my dressing room to await the legendary Stephen Sondheim and be the recipient of his even more legendary "notes" on my performance. As I waited alone for that knock on my door, I had a few moments to ponder the extraordinary significance of the moment I was living in: about to make my lifetime dream of performing on a Broadway stage come true. It was mind-blowing to me.

Stephen arrived and graciously praised my performance, giving me (blessedly) just a few benign notes.

"That's it?" I asked him, incredulously.

"That's it," he responded. "Just show up."

And then I said to him, "You know, Stephen, even if I never get to make my Broadway debut, I will have gotten from this experience everything I could have ever dreamed."

He nodded. "Because you did the work."

I debuted on December 7, 1999, to the best reviews of my life. Something I wasn't used to at all, believe me.

What is your lifetime dream?

Have you accomplished it? If not, what work must you do to make your dream come true?

A Velvet Rut

*O*n December 8, 1999, executive producer Rob Burnett called me and asked me to be the first woman to host *Late Night with David Letterman.*

I was stunned but flattered. I said something like, "You bet your ass, mister."

After hosting the Letterman show, I knew without a doubt I was to move on from *Live with Regis and Kathie Lee* and into a whole new season of my creative life. I remember clearly hearing the Lord's voice above the audience's applause after my monologue. "Take a mental picture, Kathie," He said to me. "This is the moment your life changed."

The next day I told Regis. Hard as it was for both of us, he understood. Then I announced my decision on the air on Monday.

People think you're either crazy or incredibly ungrateful when you walk away from that kind of success. I was neither. I was totally grateful for the unprecedented opportunity I had had with Regis and equally grateful for the thrilling yet unknown opportunities that awaited me.

I *had* to leave. Artists die on the vine unless they are creating, and I had already squeezed every ounce of creative juice I had out of my fifteen amazing years with my dear friend and partner.

I had been in a velvet rut: making TV history, making a boatload of money, yet dying inside to get to those big-bucket dreams. It was time. So I walked away in July 2000 to an unknown but exciting future.

But nothing ever actually turns out the way you think it will, does it?

Sometimes it's even better.

Think about your own hopes and dreams. Is there something you've put up on a shelf, telling yourself, "Maybe someday" or "I could never do that . . ."? It might be time to dust that thing off and take another look. Or maybe, like me, you find yourself in a velvet rut that simply makes it too easy to stay. Give yourself the gift of dreaming.

Have you walked away from something because
you knew it was time for a new beginning? What
did you leave behind? What was next for you?

Why do you think it is hard for people to understand
that it's okay to walk away from success?

The Future

I hate the phrase *reinvent yourself*. And I'm not fond of the word *retire*. I prefer re-*fire*. For how can I reinvent myself when I never invented myself to begin with? God created me, and He created you too. Acts 17 says, "in him we live and move and have our being" (v. 28).

So when I left *Live with Regis and Kathie Lee*, I didn't retire. I moved on to the next stage of my life. I concentrated on other interests. I recorded two CDs, *Heart of a Woman* for Universal Records and *Born for You* on my own label, On the Lamb Records. The first one flopped and the second one didn't. That's the yin and yang and ebb and flow of the business.

I continued my work in theater and opened the musical *Under the Bridge* at the Zipper Theatre in 2005.

I've learned that you can't allow other people to write the story that God has already written for you. We must believe that your future is going to be better than your past—and most importantly your past doesn't define you. We all endure hopeless situations, but we must turn to God and listen obediently so he can show up for us.

You must have an open heart for the future and what is

beyond your vision. Moreover, we must have faith by shifting our sight so we can see the good, the blessings, and the life in every circumstance.

When you're taking the next steps and turning the page to another chapter, don't allow yourself to think of the next steps as reinventing yourself because you already have the gifts and talents within you.

What do you think about the phrase *reinvent yourself*? Has your opinion of this phrase shifted since reading this?

How do you know when it is time to take next steps in your future? Are there specific signs you look for? Do you listen to God?

Don't Believe Everything

I have learned to never believe what you hear or read about someone. The media is generated by an insatiable lust for power, prestige, and most importantly, money.

The first real professional song I ever wrote, called "You Sell," was a commentary on this theme. I performed it at the Rainbow Room at the top of Rockefeller Center for two weeks in my cabaret act and also in my monologue when I hosted *Late Night with David Letterman*.

The tabloids wrote all kinds of garbage about me because, for some inexplicable reason, I sold millions of dollars of magazines and newspapers for them.

The tabloids only exist because there's a huge, voracious appetite in our culture to consume garbage. We put trash in our bodies every day in the form of junk food. We also put trash into our minds when we purchase salacious and unsubstantiated gossip. It doesn't really matter if any of it is true or not; all that matters is that it sells. And it will sell until the next person arrives on the scene and it starts all over again under a new name.

If I hadn't been able to hold on to my own truth through all the viciousness of those years, I'd be in the Betty Ford

Center, or in prison, or dead. But I didn't let the headlines define me. I battled every day to keep reminding myself that only God could do that. And every day I clung for dear life to what His Word said about me.

I have known many of the people who have been swept up in the headlines over the last four decades. Many I consider friends; others are colleagues. It has pained me to watch how the lies have damaged some of their reputations and livelihoods. In cases when I knew the accusations to be true, I was pleased to see them brought to justice.

Many innocent people have been destroyed, and too many truly guilty people are still walking around freely, continuing to use their power to abuse others. It's infuriating, isn't it? I understand why so many scream at their radios and TVs, lashing out at all the insanity.

There is something very basic and primal in us that longs for justice. But that, too, has been perverted in our culture. Because if we don't care about justice *for all*, we don't really care about it *at all*, do we?

My point is this: I continue to believe in the truth about the people I have known personally and privately. And that truth has rarely been what I heard or read anywhere else.

In life we hear rumors or believe everything we
see on social media, and we prematurely formulate

an opinion. When was the last time you were surprised by someone or something you unfairly judged? Did you apologize for your misjudgment?

What do you think about the statement, "If we don't care about justice *for all*, we don't really care about it *at all*"?

DAY 22

Everyday Blessings

I was born in Paris, France, but my parents weren't the least bit French, so neither am I. We were in France because my daddy was in the navy. He had been assigned a position with General Dwight D. Eisenhower's staff at SHAPE (Supreme Headquarters Allied Powers Europe).

My parents had never been to Europe, so they embraced everything they experienced while they were there—all of the European traditions as well as traveling every chance they had to explore the wonders of England, Germany, Italy, and Switzerland. When they finally did return to America, they brought their memories and their newfound affection for the delicacies they had discovered. Most especially, wine.

I grew up in this environment. I have wonderful memories of watching them enjoy a bottle of Chianti with my mother's spaghetti or a classic chardonnay with her roasted chicken. I associate wine with beautiful family memories, which has had a profound effect on my own sensibilities about the abundant life.

Wine is the most commonly mentioned alcoholic beverage in the Bible. It is a source of symbolism, yes, but it was also a deeply important part of Judaic life during biblical times. Interestingly, the ancient Hebrews also drank beer,[2] just like my daddy discovered when he was transferred from Paris to Wiesbaden, Germany.

We had a loving home with parents who celebrated God's blessings every day. It was joyful, it was celebratory, and it was fun. So when I was given the opportunity to partner with a successful company called Scheid Family Wines, I was very excited. I named my wines GIFFT not only because it contains letters from my own name but also as a play on the word *gift*—which I believe all blessings are.

Do you have any special memories or
celebrations that include a bottle of wine?

How do you celebrate God's blessings every day?

A Man Among Men

*F*rank had a strong, deeply rooted religious upbringing. His parents were Pentecostal Christians, and every time they moved to a new place, they found the closest Assembly of God church and put their three children in Sunday school.

Weldon Gifford, Frank's father, was an oil worker and often out of work. It was the 1930s, and the Great Depression had ravaged many a family all over the country. The Giffords moved twenty-nine times. We know this from Frank's mother's Bible, which chronicled every move. It was a bleak and difficult time for them—even having to, at times, eat dog food to survive. But they were grateful for it.

Every time the family moved Frank would establish himself in the new community with his athletic prowess.

The family finally settled in Bakersfield, California, when Frank was in high school. He was the youngest of the three children and the first Gifford to graduate from high school, much less graduate from college—which he did as an All-American Trojan football player at the University of Southern California.

Always an athlete, Frank played football every chance he got. His high school grades weren't strong enough to gain the athletic scholarship he needed for college, so he attended Bakersfield Junior College, played a season of football there, and got his grades up to what was required for him to enroll at USC.

A man among men, Frank grew up believing in a big, all-powerful God of the universe, but he never understood what it meant to have a personal relationship with the living God. Not until we went to Israel in 2012 with our dear friends Emilie and Craig Wierda (who are now Cassidy's in-laws). That experience changed everything for Frank. He got baptized in the Jordan River he'd heard so much about back in Sunday school decades before.

Frank, who had also come to know Jesus late in his extraordinary life, came home from Israel a changed man. He'd often say to me, "You know what, honey, I'm not afraid to die. I'm actually starting to get very curious." And though no one ever wants to talk about their own death, he told me many times that he did not want to be buried. He was claustrophobic. "Don't put me in a box," he'd insist. "And promise you'll pull the plug if anyone starts to wipe my buns."

I'd always chuckle and say, "Frank, I love you very much, but I'm not going to go to prison for you."

"Then just trip over it and make it look like an accident."

He also was very clear that he did not want a funeral. He

hated funerals. He buried way too many people he loved in his almost eighty-five years.

"Just throw me a big party in the backyard, serve GIFFT wine, and blare Sinatra. And only invite people I actually care about. No assholes. Oh, and don't let anyone tell sad stories and start crying. Only funny ones."

He died on a Sunday morning in 2015 one week shy of his eighty-fifth birthday. Three days later we threw him a party—exactly the kind he wanted.

Were you raised in a religious family? Do you have a personal relationship with the living God?

If you do, was there a specific moment when your relationship with God became real and changed you?

DAY 24

An Infamous Daredevil

*O*ne of the most colorful misfits I've ever met is Evel Knievel, the infamous daredevil who defied gravity and sanity but kept the world breathless with his exploits. He and Frank were good friends.

Evel's career had made him a media and cultural darling. I really liked Evel—I appreciated his uniqueness and his honesty.

Most of the time the subject of our conversations would turn to religion. I tried unsuccessfully for years to convince Evel that I hated the baggage that comes with organized religion, and I attempted to steer him to other more positive aspects, but he was better at talking than listening.

He would launch into a diatribe about his kids, his ex-wives, doctors, or the media—whatever it happened to be that had infuriated him that particular day.

It always ended the same way, with me saying, "Evel, I'm praying for you. Lots of people who love you are praying for you, and one day you're going to call me out of the blue and say, 'Kathie, you're right! I don't hate Jesus, I *love* Him.'" And then he'd laugh and hang up the phone.

I answered the phone one day to hear Evel's familiar voice literally screaming, "Kathie! You were right! I accepted Jesus. He's real, and He loves me. Let me talk to Frank!"

It was surreal. Evel got on the phone with Frank and talked his ear off about his real-life leap—but this was one of faith. Frank was tickled by it.

"Kath," he said afterward, "did I ever tell you about Evel's worst jump?"

"No. What happened?"

"It was in London in 1975 at Wembley Stadium. He was supposed to jump over thirteen buses. The night before the telecast we walked into the stadium to survey the site. There were the thirteen buses lined up. Evel looked at the ramp for a long time. Then he looked at me and said, 'Frank, I can't do it. I can make it over twelve but not thirteen.'

"I asked him, 'Are you sure, Evel?'

"'Yep,' he said, as if it were the most natural thing in the world.

"'Well, Evel, if you're sure you can't make it, you have to cancel the jump.'

"'No, I can't cancel,' he said. 'But I can't make the jump.'"

"Frank!" I shouted in the middle of the story. "Why not?"

"''Cause he said he'd do it. That was Evel."

"What happened?" I asked, almost afraid to know.

"He didn't make it. Exactly as he said would happen. He hit the thirteenth bus and went flying in the air for yards. People thought he was dead. But as they carried him out of the stadium, he lifted up his arm and the crowd went wild. I rushed over to him, and as I leaned in he grabbed me and pulled me close. Obviously concerned about more than how his latest stunt had ended, Evel said, 'Frank, get that broad out of my hotel room.'"

It was one of Frank's all-time favorite stories to tell. Not only was it classic Evel Knievel, it was proof that anyone can make a leap of faith.

Have you taken a leap of faith?
What pushed you to do it?

Do you have a friend like Evel Knievel? If so, what are
your favorite memories you've shared together?

Everybody Has a Story

I love stories. Everyone has them, and it's a gift to listen to others tell theirs. People come alive when they share their stories. And they feel validated that someone wants to hear them.

You want to feel *really* good? Go into a nursing home or a hospital and ask the people you meet to tell you their story. For some of them—and probably way too many—it will be the first time anyone has asked. And, oh, what stories most *all* of them have to tell.

When I first joined *TODAY* it was with the understanding that I would be allowed to bring my love for theater—which is actually storytelling—to a live television audience. I'm grateful to our executive producer at the time, Jim Bell, for honoring that commitment.

My desire was to have a monthly segment called "Everyone Has a Story" in which our viewers would submit their personal accounts and we would choose one to turn into a song. Then we would welcome the viewer to our sofa and perform the song that my writing partner, David Friedman, and I had created. Sung by the greatest singers in the world: Broadway stars!

In eleven years we wrote one hundred "Everyone Has a Story" songs and saw one hundred ordinary people with extraordinary lives respond in real time. It was a total joy and privilege to bring these unique experiences to life.

We are wired to share stories because our Father created us to connect. Learning more about someone and what shapes them allows us to understand them on a different—deeper—level. Giving someone the space to share their story adds value and nourishment to relationships. By listening you're telling that person they are validated, worthy, and matter. At the end of the day, when it is all said and done, everyone wants to feel like their life was meaningful.

Do you enjoy listening to other people tell their stories? How has hearing about someone else's story impacted your life?

What would your "Everyone Has a Story" song
sound like? What things would you highlight?

DAY 26

Love Changes Everything

My parents' life stories were heartbreaking but ultimately triumphant, as all the best ones are.

Both of my parents' childhoods were like Dickens novels—child abandoned, child abused, child unloved, and child left hopeless until . . . love showed up and changed everything.

My father's Russian/Jewish immigrant father abandoned his wife and five young children. He drank too much and ran around too much—an all-too-common tale then and now.

My mother's mother died of tuberculosis when my mom was two, followed a year later by my mother's only brother, who died from measles. The stock market had crashed, and my mother's father had lost his fortune and successful career in publishing. He, too, took to alcohol to numb the pain and soon married an equally wounded woman who shared his addictions. Once a classical violinist, my maternal grandfather descended into a haze of despair ending in frequent booze-fueled fights with his wife and trips to jail in the "paddy wagon." My mom, Joanie, and her sister, Marilyn, had to go in the paddy wagon as well because there was no one to care for them.

My grandfather died when my mother was nine years old. Joanie's sense of shame was born of such events. Her whole life she would battle a profound but deeply embedded lie in her soul: she wasn't loved, she wasn't good enough, and she was unworthy of happiness. Her grandmother was the only light in her broken life.

Quite old already and crippled with rheumatoid arthritis in her feet, my great-grandmother struggled to care for her two young granddaughters and teach them how to survive in such a heartless, brutally unfair world. Then she, too, died when Joanie was fifteen. Marilyn had married young and moved away. Joanie was truly alone in the world.

Because of this, Joanie had to drop out of school and go to work at the local five-and-dime store, living in her one and only girlfriend's house and forced to give almost every cent she earned to the friend's mother to help pay the rent. Into this hopelessness, love arrived in the form of a lanky, athletic, hardworking young naval petty officer, my daddy, Eppie Epstein.

My dad literally rescued my mom from that house and took her home to his. His family rejected her, too, but Daddy loved and protected her for the next fifty-four years.

Broken upbringings are very common. How do you think tough circumstances impact a person's mental health? How can broken upbringings shift things in a positive direction for the future?

Do you believe in soulmates? Do you think there is someone for everyone? Why or why not?

DAY 27

Amazing Grace

*M*y daddy's father, Meyer "Sam" Epstein, was a complicated man. Although he was by all accounts a terrible husband and father, he had a reputation as a warm and generous man to the neediest in his neighborhood. I can't imagine what my daddy had to do to reconcile his father's coldness and emotional abuse with the outpouring of affection his father displayed to total strangers.

Sam Epstein was a Jew by birth and heritage, but he was

not a religious man. My father's mother, Evelyn, was not religious either. But one very hot and sticky summer day, when my father was eight, she sent all five of her children to the church down the street when she had reached her limit and couldn't take any more of their rowdiness.

That's how my father found himself at Vacation Bible School asking Jesus into his heart. Seven years later, when he was walking around the Maryland State House in Annapolis, a gang of young hooligans attacked him, throwing rocks at him and screaming, "Christ killer! Christ killer! Christ killer!" It breaks my heart now to think of the terrible confusion my father had to live with because of his last name and heritage.

When my dad was fourteen years old, he went to work and gave all the money he made to his mother so she could buy an old used car. Evelyn eventually married again, only to lose her husband, David, and her oldest son, Paul, in World War II. Her middle son, Carol (pronounced Carl), was wounded. Only my daddy returned home from the war unscathed physically, but he was deeply affected emotionally.

Unlike Mom, Daddy never spoke of the past. He suffered privately and stoically. He was incredibly healthy—I only saw him get one cold in all the years I knew and loved him. He worked hard every day of his life and helped everyone who asked him for it, and many who didn't.

One day when I was quite young I remember hearing my parents whispering about Sam Epstein. Apparently, he was gravely ill in a hospital in Baltimore, asking for his children to come to his bedside. My father was the only one who went. Mom later told us that Daddy stood by his father's bed and lovingly held his hand.

"Forgive me, son," his father whispered.

"I forgive you, Pop," is all my daddy said as his father died.

I believe with all my heart that God saw my daddy in that hospital room that day. He saw all the woundedness and hurt inside of him. And God shed a tear when my daddy extended mercy to the man who had never given it in return. Grace . . . amazing grace.

Have you extended grace to someone unexpectedly?
If not, has someone extended you grace when
you thought it was impossible to do so?

Do you believe that grace can set someone free
from grief and bitterness? Why or why not?

A Lovely Woman

My father, Eppie, was diagnosed with Lewy body dementia and began an eight-year nightmare of mental and physical deterioration. He died after eight days in hospice at home on November 19, 2002. My mother had just been reciting the Twenty-third Psalm for the umpteenth time when he suddenly lifted up, opened his eyes, let out a deep breath, and settled peacefully back onto his pillow.

Mom was a widow for the next fifteen years. Eventually we had to move her into an assisted living facility called Baywoods on the banks of the Severn River in Annapolis, where my daddy had been born and had grown into a great man.

She lived for her family's visits, Hallmark movies, and her biblical archaeological magazines. Everyone was her friend. She lit up every room she went into and stopped to talk (endlessly!) with anyone she happened to encounter in her tiny, sheltered world. She maintained her childlike love for Jesus, which had been born of great suffering. She knew Him intimately, for she knew deep in her soul that He had saved her life by sacrificing His.

Mom could no longer travel to visit my brother and me

up north, so Dave and I began monthly visits to see her in Annapolis.

I lost count of the trips, but I treasure the memory of the long rides my adorable brother and I would take on the train from New York and the early morning talks with my sister, who had long ago taken on the full-time job of caretaker to our parents.

Late in August 2017, after a family visit, we returned to Baywoods. The night nurse greeted Mom with great joy and promised she'd be in soon to give Mom her medications. It always made me sad to change Mom out of her clothes and into her nightgown, robe, and slippers. How many times had she done that for all of us when we were little? I hated leaving her there alone, although of course she wasn't there alone at all. She said she always felt her Eppie next to her and the Lord, who she knew without a doubt would never leave her side.

I settled Mom into her cozy chair and began to put on her slippers. Mom had always been beautiful, a true world-class lovely woman. But she had inherited her grandmother's feet, and by age eighty-seven, it seemed that every toe lived in a different zip code. I don't know why the sight of them this particular time broke my heart.

How does she even walk on them, Lord? I silently prayed and loved on her with all my goodbyes while fighting tears. We would always linger with her, but eventually, we had to leave.

That night I prayed, "Oh, please, Jesus, take Mommy home. Let her run on two perfect feet right into Your loving arms."

Two weeks later, God answered my prayer. Mom died peacefully in her sleep and woke up with Jesus, her Eppie, her mother, her father, her brother, her sister, and her precious grandmother who had loved her and cared for her with those incredibly painful, crippled feet. Now, Nana's feet were perfect too.

Do you know someone who has a childlike
love for Jesus? If so, what can you learn or
have you learned from this person?

Have you ever prayed for a loved one to go home to
Jesus because you knew that's where they wanted to
be? How did you prepare your heart to let go? Is there
something you wish you had told them before they left?

New Friends

*I*n January 2016 the State of Israel requested that NBC allow me to come to the Holy Land to tape a series for Holy Week, and NBC agreed. Tourism had been suffering due to reports of terrorism in the news, and they felt that I would be able to quell some of the fears.

I have been traveling to Israel since I was seventeen. My dad gifted me a trip as my high school graduation present. I feel safer in Israel than anywhere I've ever been. The Israelis are better at security than anyone. They have to be because their survival depends on it.

As the crew began to set up, our very fine producer, Yael Federbush, suggested that I go and dance with some of the young female teenagers who were in front of the Western Wall. I'm not sure if it was the noise levels or all the twirling around; I heard something pop, and my head began to pound.

I've been blessed with incredible health, energy, and stamina my whole life, but this was terrifying beyond anything that had ever happened to me. Someone handed me some acetaminophen, but it never came close to dulling the pain.

I do not know how I managed to stay upright and do my

stand-up and interview there at the wall, but God got me through it. I went back to the hotel hoping I'd feel better but I didn't.

I got ready for the next shoot and went down to meet Yael in the lobby. The next two days were a complete blur to me: camera settings, shots, stand-ups, and interviews.

Eventually we were climbing a steep mountain to overlook the celebrated valley where David defeated Goliath. I was finally feeling better and was looking forward to reaching the summit.

I never made it. Halfway up the mountain, and halfway through filming the setup as we climbed, I felt another pop in my ears and fell to the ground with the same excruciating pain. The crew car took me to a hospital.

Yael had called ahead to arrange immediate admission. I was taken to a private room and put on a bed to await a series of tests. I was grateful to lie down.

The door opened and a young man entered. His name was Nurse Jihad, which, I'll admit, made me a bit uneasy. But his eyes were kind and his voice was gentle as he proceeded to take out his stethoscope and, with calmness and professionalism, begin to review my symptoms, and later direct me through the grueling set of tests that were ordered.

My twelve-hour ordeal ended with a spinal tap five thousand miles away from home but not friendless. I finished the shoot and packed for my return to New York City thinking,

This is the Israel we never hear about. This is the Israel I know and love.

I will always be grateful for the sweet man who took care of me—a Muslim man working side by side with Jews, saving the lives of any and every person who came through their doors, including me—regardless of our race, religion, nationality, or gender.

You never know where you might meet a new friend. Keep an open mind (and heart) because they often come how and when you least expect it.

When was the last time you were pleasantly surprised by someone because you had an open mind and open heart? How did that experience change future interactions?

Have you missed out on an experience or a connection with someone because you had a closed mind? If you did, what did you miss?

Faith of a Mustard Seed

A motley group of both family and friends came with me on the NBC series filming trip to Israel to study rabbinically. I didn't want to take only believers, so I asked the Lord to reveal who He wanted to go. One by one they responded: a Sikh, a Hindu, Scientologists, an atheist, an agnostic, brokenhearted Catholics, two Navy SEALs, and a couple of confused Baptists. Plus my kids and Cody's girlfriend, Erika, and Frank's daughter, Vicki.

One by one I watched each person begin to relax and lean into Rod VanSolkema's teaching.

I loved watching the Word of God wash over this special group of men and women from different cultures and faiths. They truly looked to me like the kingdom of God.

By the end of the trip it was obvious that everyone had been impacted in a life-transforming way. Most everyone was baptized in the Jordan River, but every single member of our insula (family) gathered together on our last morning to take communion in the garden of Gethsemane.

Watching my children being baptized in the Jordan River was one of the highlights of my life. After I left the baptism site to secure a car for a member of our group who needed assistance, I heard one final splash along with cheers from our group.

What? I thought. *What was that?* I believed everyone who wanted to had already been baptized. But I was wrong.

On the Wednesday after Frank died, once we had celebrated his extraordinary life in our backyard, we had a family prayer time at Praise Point—Frank's favorite place on our property.

We each took some of his ashes and had our private moments of remembrance of the beloved man we already missed. On our way back up to the house I said to Vicki, his daughter, "You need to know that your daddy died a very contented man. He was at peace. The last few years of his life, since he went to Israel, he kept saying to me, 'I'm not afraid of dying, honey. I'm actually getting really curious.'"

Vicki was understandably heartbroken and trying to process yet another devastating loss in her life. But there was one more thing I knew I had to tell her.

"Even so, there was one thing that still concerned him."

"What?" she asked.

"You, sweetie. You're his only child who still doesn't know Jesus. He wanted you to have that peace in your life too."

That next year, while on the trip to Israel, my sweet friend Anne Neilson saw Vicki sitting on a rock and sobbing as each member of our insula went into the Jordan River to be baptized.

"I want to go in there," she said through her tears, "but I don't have enough faith."

Anne's tender heart broke for her. "You've seen all the beautiful mustard seed plants everywhere?" she said.

"Yes."

"Vicki, the mustard seed starts out as the tiniest seed in all of botany. Yet nothing can destroy it once it takes hold and begins to grow. Honey, that's all you need to get you in the water. Just the faith of a mustard seed. Do you have that much?"

"Yes," she said, "I do."

After almost thirty years of sharing the hope of the Savior with her to no avail, that beautiful day at the Jordan River she surrendered to all she didn't yet understand and fell back into the arms of Pastor Rod and our dear Navy SEAL friend, Remi Adeleke.

Do you have faith the size of a mustard seed? How has that tiny seed of faith impacted your life?

Have you been baptized? What is your baptism story?

All for Good

*A*fter a trip to Israel alongside the NBC team, the Israeli Ministry of Tourism office in New York reached out to me with a proposition. They wanted me to be the face of Israel in all of North America.

My heart leapt. I'd been praying for something like this for years.

"Gentlemen," I began, "I don't even have to pray about this! This is all I've wanted to do since I was twelve years old."

They were obviously pleased until I said this: "But I'm going to say something now that you've probably never heard before." I paused. "You can't pay me one penny for it. I want to be able to sit with any publication and say honestly that I have never received a dime of compensation for performing these services. That my actions have all been completely done out of my love for God's land and His people."

They looked at each other incredulously.

I smiled at them and said, "That doesn't mean it isn't going to cost you something."

Now I had their attention.

"I want people to visit Israel—the Holy Land—and study

rabbinically so that they come to an understanding of the power of God's original Word in the Greek and Hebrew."

They nodded that they understood.

"So every time I come for you to represent the State of Israel, I want you to sponsor fifty pastors or seminary students to come with me—to study alongside me. Then when they return to America, they will take with them a profound new excitement about their relationship with Yeshua and exponentially share it with others." They instantly and eagerly agreed, so we spent the rest of our time together discussing the possibilities. Until week after week passed with little or no word from the Israeli Ministry of Tourism office.

Our lunch meeting was in late March. Immediately afterward I had contacted the King's University in Dallas, Texas, to organize the fifty students and pastors that they deemed most deserving of a ten-day, all-expense-paid rabbinical trip to Israel. They were thrilled and soon the departure day arrived—without one word from the tourism board and not one penny in the coffers to pay for their trips.

I felt I had no choice but to pay the entire amount. I couldn't disappoint all of these people whose dreams of studying in the Holy Land were about to come true. I was very sad about the obvious miscommunication between us, but I made no mention of it publicly.

Though it was hurtful, I tried not to let bitterness take root in my heart. I convinced myself that God would use it all for good. And in time, of course, that's exactly what He did. Later, I received letters from every one of the students, who shared how blessed they had been, how they were individually affected in a positive way by the experience, and how they planned to share their education with others. This was the end that I'd hoped for and the answer to the specific prayers that I finally *did* pray.

Fifty pilgrims went to Israel that fall and came back transformed individuals.

Have you experienced disappointment that forced you to remind yourself that God would use it all for good? How did that belief allow you to shift your mindset?

Have you ever allowed bitterness to take root in your heart? What happened? What would you change or do differently?

Strangers

*P*eople come and go in our lives. Some are soon forgotten, but others make an indelible imprint. Then there are those few who are game changers, and finally, there are the life changers.

Hoda Kotb and I were in Nashville for our show and the producers booked a segment for the show where we were going to sit in a "writer's room" with one of the best song-writers in town, Brett James, and try to write a song together.

Brett and I ended up writing the song in thirty seconds, which made for a very entertaining segment. As we were packing up our gear, Brett said, "Kathie, I was a big fan of your husband. I'm so sorry you lost him. How are you and your kids doing?"

"We're doing fine, Brett. Truly. I found him that morning and his face was wide with wonder. He saw Jesus, and Jesus took his breath away. And someday I'm going to write that song."

Brett didn't hesitate. "Well, then, let's write that song."

"Okay," I said, actually thinking, *Sure we will*. I wrote down my number and he said he'd call me to make a plan.

Twenty minutes later in the car my phone rang. It was

Brett. We made plans to get together the next week at his studio to write the song.

I had never sat down to write a song with someone who was pretty much a complete stranger. And since I had no idea what to expect, I wrote four lines to give us a starting point: "A little kiss. A little coffee. A little moment to pray. Our Sunday mornings always started that way."

Brett smiled. "Well, that's how we're going to start our song," he said. We finished it in all of twenty minutes and titled it "He Saw Jesus."

We spent the better part of the day talking and getting to know each other, then I headed for home. Brett flew to my house in Connecticut a couple of weeks later to record the demo in my studio. "You know I don't sing professionally anymore," I kept saying. "I damaged my vocal cords nearly fourteen years ago because of a bad case of pneumonia. My daddy was in hospice for such a short time, and I didn't want to leave and go to the doctor. I've lost thirty percent of my breathing capacity."

"Uh-huh," he said. "You'll be great. I'll protect you in the booth."

He was infuriatingly calm even as I was growing more terrified by the moment. "No, Brett, I'm serious. Who are we going to get to actually sing it?"

"We'll talk about that later," he said, nonchalantly. "Right now, let's just get your vocal down and then start working on the next song."

I struggled through the demo session. It was strange to be so insecure about a gift I had taken for granted for forty years. An hour later Brett was convinced we had a great demo of "He Saw Jesus," so we wrapped our session and went upstairs to start a brand-new song that eventually became "Once Again."

I performed "He Saw Jesus" on the *TODAY* show and within fifteen seconds it went to number one on iTunes. Just try to outdo God. It was a very creative time for me—something I realized was both healing and energizing as I stepped into the next phase of my life.

Has a complete stranger ever pleasantly surprised you and become an integral part of your next chapter? If so, who and how?

Has a creative experience turned out to be one of healing and renewed energy? If so, what happened, and how did it impact your life?

Closure

_B_rett James and his daughter, Clare, spent the weekend in New York going to two Tony Award–winning musicals. Afterward they came to visit me in my home in Connecticut. Brett asked if he could hear some of the score to the Broadway musical _Scandalous_ that I had written many years prior. My heart stopped. I hadn't been able to listen to a note of the cast album since the show had closed more than four years earlier. It was still too painful.

Scandalous, which first ran under the title _Saving Aimee_, is the story of the life and career of evangelist and pop-culture icon Aimee Semple McPherson. The music was written with David Pomeranz, David Friedman, and me and featured songs such as "Stand Up!" "I Have a Fire," and "For Such a Time as This." Carolee Carmello, the extraordinary and brilliant leading lady, went on to receive a Tony Award nomination for Best Leading Actress in a Musical for her portrayal of McPherson. She gave the finest performance I have ever seen by any Broadway actress. When she was nominated, we felt like we all were.

"I guess I could play you one song," I told Brett, though I was not sure I actually could.

"No, I want to hear the whole thing."

I gulped and went to find the CD. Minutes later, over dinner in my garden, I watched them as they listened. Clare was seventeen years old at the time—the exact age that Aimee is when the musical begins. By the third song Clare said, "Daddy, this is so much better than anything we saw this weekend."

"It is, honey," he agreed.

My heart soared.

After five songs Brett put down his fork, leaned back in his chair, and closed his eyes. When he opened them, he looked at me and said, "You wrote this? Every word?"

"Yes," I told him honestly, "and forty more songs that didn't make the cut."

He responded by saying one word, and in doing so, gave me the single greatest compliment I have ever been paid in my entire career. I won't share it here because it's too embarrassing, but believe me when I tell you, it changed my entire perspective on the incredibly agonizing Broadway experience. Once again I found the gift of closure, like when Brett and I wrote and recorded "He Saw Jesus." This time it was closure from all of the pain I had experienced during the thirteen years it took to write and produce *Scandalous*.

Sometimes God heals you in the blink of an eye; more often it seems to take forever. The beauty in the long road is that He will often use someone else to be a part of your healing.

What memories have you locked away
because they are too painful to share?

Who has God used to be part of your healing? Have you
developed a relationship with this person, or was this person
only meant to be part of a specific season in your life?

DAY 34

Dreams

I didn't choose this journey I'm on.
This journey was chosen for me.
I didn't ask for this task I've been given,
And I'd give it up, gratefully.
If I could
I would.
But I won't.
I can't.
All of the broken lives, and all of the broken dreams
Coming down the aisles in steady streams.

—"For Such a Time as This"
by Kathie Lee Gifford, from *Scandalous*

It seems some dreams are like that. No matter what you do, or how hard you work, they sometimes simply run themselves right out of time to become what you had imagined they would be. It's true for all of us.

Still, dead ends don't have to be the end of dreaming. And they're certainly not the end of opportunities that lie ahead. It is important to remember—especially when you're actively dreaming—following your dreams isn't easy and dreamers are usually not in love with the process that it takes to achieve everything. Reality will always be messy. Trials and tribulations are part of life, and there's no way around them.

Knowing that there will be brokenness shouldn't sway you to not pursue your dreams. Just remember that everything is part of the journey—the good, the bad, and the in between. God has a plan for all of His children, and instead of trying to take control of the story He's written, you must be willing to enjoy the ride.

What dreams have you had that shifted
into something completely different?

What dead ends have you encountered, and
how did you overcome the obstacles?

Love and Marriage

I wrote a song with Phil Sillas for Billy and Ruth Graham to celebrate their extraordinary marriage, which lasted over sixty years. "Our Loving Eyes" tells the story of a legacy of living through the ups and downs of life together and ends with this picture of their beautiful, extraordinary love:

No need to speak of all we share.
It comes as no surprise
That we'll continue our sweet romance
With our eyes, our loving eyes.

No need to speak of all we feel.
We know what's true, we know what's real.
And until we whisper the last of our goodbyes
We'll continue our romance
With our loving eyes.

We dreamed our dreams together, we walked the narrow road,
Shared every burden side by side.
And as we turned each corner, we turned to God above,
Depending on His grace to sanctify our love.

Now we sit by the fire,
Weathered by the years,
Strengthened by the trials,
Tendered by the tears.

Billy and Ruth had a beautiful union together. Billy once said, "Ruth and I don't have a perfect marriage, but we have a great one." He went on to say, "In a perfect marriage, everything is always the finest and best imaginable; like a Greek statue, the proportions are exact and the finish is unblemished. Who knows any human beings like that?"

My dear friend was right. Marriage doesn't have to be perfect to be great. "Love is patient and kind; love does not envy or boast; it is not arrogant or rude. It does not insist on its own way; it is not irritable or resentful; it does not rejoice at wrongdoing, but rejoices with the truth"[3] (1 Corinthians 13:4–6 ESV).

Do you know an extraordinary love that's lasted
through ups and downs? Who is the couple? What
have you learned from their everlasting bond?

Marriages, statistically, have a fifty-fifty chance of survival.
Why do you think half of couples decide to end their
marriage instead of continuing to do life together?

Thank You, Forever

The world's loss on February 21, 2018, was heaven's gain. That was the day Billy Graham left this world at the age of ninety-nine to enter into his greatest eternal adventure. I was sitting in the makeup chair at NBC that morning when the news came over the wires. I immediately raised my face and lifted my arms to the skies and said, "Thank You, Jesus." I truly believe that no one in history has ever personally been responsible for so many millions of people coming to faith in Jesus.

I had known Billy since I was in my early twenties and had been immeasurably blessed to be counted among his friends.

My mind went back to 1996 when Frank and I had attended the ceremony at the Capitol where Billy and his magnificent wife, Ruth, both received a Congressional Gold Medal—the highest honor the government can give a civilian. We loved sharing this moment with them. Ruth was extremely ill at the time and sat in a wheelchair next to the podium, never speaking as person after person rose up to exalt the honorees.

When it had been Billy's turn to address the audience

assembled in that esteemed and time-honored place in history, there was not a sound to be heard. He looked around at the busts of treasured heroes featured in the rotunda and gestured for us to see and consider them too.

"They have one thing in common: they're all dead. And we're going to join them. . . . If ever we needed God's help, it is now. If ever we needed spiritual renewal, it is now. And it can begin today in each one of our lives as we repent before God and yield ourselves to Him and His Word. What are you as an individual going to do?"[4]

I have so many fond memories of Billy that I'll never forget. I remember coming to faith in Jesus in a movie theater when I was twelve years old while watching the Billy Graham film *The Restless Ones*. I remember him coming to my house in Connecticut in November 1994 to tape my Christmas special and wanting a Big Mac.

He was also the first person to call me when I was falsely accused of operating sweatshops and after it was revealed that Frank had cheated on me and broken my heart.

I remember the look on Frank's face when I passed the phone to him after the news of the infidelity broke. I watched as Billy's words of mercy and grace washed over him. I could see his eyes well up with tears as he heard Billy's magnificent voice tell him, "Remember, Frank, there is now no condemnation in Christ. We all have sinned and fallen short of the glory of God."

"Thank you, Billy," was all Frank could say.

So, I'll say it again for all of us:
Thank you, Billy Graham. Thank you. Forever.

Has Billy Graham impacted your life? Did one of his books inspire you? Did a sermon speak directly to you?

The renewal of the mind involves a transformation of the way a person thinks and lives. Do you practice spiritual renewal? If so, what do you do?

DAY 37

Just Be You

God is full of surprises. Sometimes He surprises us with the brand-new way a story reveals itself, which can inspire us to new heights of creativity—that is, if we're not afraid to go there and not afraid of what anyone will think.

I believe it is important to not have a religion but a relationship with God. That relationship will change your life because it will not only guide you, but it will nurture you. I say all this because sometimes the world can feel dark and scary. Horrible things are said and done every day—and in many cases we don't even know if we're hearing or reading the truth.

We are quick to judge other people because they don't look like we do, or they don't believe everything that we believe. We are quick to cancel people because they don't go to our church or worship the way we worship.

Jesus went out to where the people were and approached the unlovable and loved them. He didn't make the people clean up their act. He didn't beg them to change or fit into a box. He believed that the Holy Spirit would do the work and that it wasn't necessary for everyone to be the same. Jesus wanted everyone to be created the way they were meant to be—which means allowing others to be who they were meant to be.

I share all of this because we must stop trying to conform people into who we think they should be. If you have feelings and emotions of disappointment or confusion, you need to take your concerns to God, and stop trying to put these positions on other people. No one should allow someone to define them—only Jesus can define you.

Has someone tried to make you change because they didn't like the way you are? Who demanded you change? How did you respond?

Have you ever forced your opinion or way of life on someone else? If yes, how did they respond? How should you have reacted? What did you learn from the experience?

More Spontaneity and Authenticity

$\mathcal{S}$o much of our culture today is manipulated, photo-shopped, and edited into sound bites. Over the years I've been asked to participate in reality shows, but I've always said no because they aren't "reality" at all. They are planned and produced and manipulated to titillate and entertain to the lowest common denominator, which usually includes some form of human degradation. I simply *cannot* watch people be devalued in any way, let alone participate in a show that promotes this.

Even though it's been twenty years since I left *Live with Regis and Kathie Lee,* people ask, "What was the secret to your success?" Regis and I always had the same answer: "Fun." Simple as that. There was not a scripted moment. We had no writers—everything was spontaneous and real. And I'm certain that is why it lasted as long and as successfully as it did. We were authentic. Love us or loathe us, viewers knew they were getting the real deal.

A part of our not being respectful of each other's humanity includes the fact that people no longer talk to each other; they scream at each other. Our dialogue has become coarse and mean-spirited. I've had to move away from this culture of hate to a culture of kindness.

What goes in must come out, right?

I'm glad I'm not on live daily television anymore, walking on political eggshells and dodging proverbial bullets. It's no fun. I'm not sure *Live with Regis and Kathie Lee* could have lasted in this social media–dominated world we live in now. We always just said whatever came to our minds. Now you have to process every thought and edit every word before you feel safe enough to actually say it. The result: no spontaneity and little authenticity. In other words, no fun.

It makes me sad for young people growing up today. How can you *find* yourself if you're not allowed to *be* yourself?

Do you watch reality TV? Do you think that reality TV contributes to the coarse and mean-spirited dialogue within our society?

How do you think social media contributes to the harshness that exists in our society? Have you had a bad social media experience?

DAY 39

Godwink

Godwinks are a series of books by my dear friend SQuire Rushnell and his wife Louise DuArt. The books contain true stories of people's experiences with what appear initially to be coincidences but in reality are moments in time when the divine aligns with the human. When God is "winking" in our lives. Interestingly, in the Hebrew language there is no word for coincidence because there is no such thing. Sovereign God is either truly sovereign in all things or not God at all.

Several years ago, we began featuring these Godwink stories on *TODAY*. They were highly rated segments, so SQuire and I took the concept to Hallmark.

It took three years to get our deal done. Initially there

was concern that an audience would be offended by the faith element, but I knew there was potentially a huge viewership just dying for wholesome, true, faith-based movies that gave them hope. We convinced Hallmark to try one and find out.

SQuire and I filmed the first movie, *A Godwink Christmas*, in Vancouver. It is based on the romantic love story of the real inn owners of the Charlotte Inn, located on the elegant island of Martha's Vineyard. My character was the determined aunt from the neighboring island of Nantucket who is right in the thick of getting the couple together. The movie was top-rated for the network and was voted by fans as their favorite inspirational Hallmark movie of the 2018 holiday season.

In 2019 we filmed *A Godwink Christmas: Meant for Love*. In this inspiring true story an amazing Godwink brought together a sweet couple, Alice and Jack, who both had given up on love. As Alice's mom, Olga, my character was the encouraging yet feisty matriarch, right in the middle of it all. IMDb called the film one of the ten best Hallmark movies of the last decade—again setting record ratings. In 2020 we released our third Hallmark script, *A Godwink Christmas: Second Chances*, and we are hoping to start making these films year-round, not just for Christmas.

SQuire and I are grateful that God would wink at us with these stories and opportunities.

Have you experienced a Godwink in your own life? How did that moment impact your life?

Have you heard a Godwink story from someone else that you found interesting or impactful?

Meet an Angel

We all desperately need angels in our lives—ethereal beings who show up "out of the blue" to bless, caress, and direct us. Especially in the deep state of loneliness I was in when I arrived in Nashville.

As far as it goes for Angie and me, think Lucy and Ethel. Or maybe Thelma and Louise. You get the picture. We have become inseparable, and I hate when I have to leave town, knowing I'm gonna miss my Angie so much. It is a genuine sisterhood. I'm deeply grateful to her and Greg, her husband, for being there for me at every turn during my life transition to Tennessee.

Angie and Greg dragged me everywhere: music festivals, clubs, church, parades (which I hate), restaurants, dinners, lunches. You name it, they dragged me there.

And something magical happened. I had fun. The show with Hoda had been fun, of course, but I hadn't had fun in my personal life for several years—actually the four years since Frank had passed. I hardly ever went out. Now I was out someplace almost every night. Or they'd be at my house just hanging out and sharing life. It's almost as if they were afraid to leave me alone. They understood my deep sense of loss and my desire to belong again, to be surrounded by sweet, like-minded souls who laugh or cry with you one minute and get down on their knees and pray for you the next.

They get me.

Angie also set up "writes" for me before I even made my move to Nashville—basically a session where songwriters get together in a room for the express purpose of writing a song.

These writes have been fascinating for me. I must have had fifty of them the first full year I was in town. Each one is completely different because the people are all so different. I love these sessions and look forward to them.

My Nashville angels, Greg and Angie, were there when I needed someone to give me a warm welcome, an encouraging word, a new fitness obsession, and a whole lot of connections.

Have you met an angel? What season of life
were you in? How did they help you?

Do you think you've been an angel to someone?
What did you do for this person? How do
you think you left this person feeling?

DAY 41
Getting Uncomfortable

*H*ow long has it been since you put on a new hat and stepped outside of your comfort zone? Because when two women who love Jesus sat down to write a song about another woman who thought nobody loved her, and when they followed in her footsteps by journeying out into the literal and metaphorical wilderness, incredible miracles took place.

In October 2018, a friend set up a write for me with artist and songwriter Nicole C. Mullen. For no apparent reason, just prior to our meeting, I'd been mindful of the biblical character of Hagar. Hagar was the Egyptian handmaiden of Sarah, Abraham's barren wife, who, after a bitter fight with Sarah, was abandoned with her son, Ishmael, in the wilderness of an area called Beersheba. It's one of the most disturbing accounts in the story of Abraham and Sarah but, like every story in the Bible, all too human.

As we began talking, I discovered that the Lord had recently placed Hagar on Nicole's heart as well. It was an easy, creative ebb and flow, and we ended our short session satisfied that we had the genesis of a solid song, which we hoped to pitch to Danny Gokey to record. We agreed that I would work on finishing the song while Nicole was traveling abroad.

A few days later, I began working on what we had written. I didn't stop with Hagar; I wrote about Ruth next, then David, and finally Mary Magdalene. Though it was not logical, I felt compelled to write it this way—a leading that I've learned to obey. Then I set it aside until Nicole and I could reconnect. It was obvious that we hadn't written a three-minute song; we had written a piece of theater, which needed a narration. Nicole was reluctant and wasn't comfortable recording but she eventually agreed. Her recording ended up being twelve minutes and was anointed by the Holy Spirit.

After very few changes to what she had both said and sung, we knew we had the final version of *The God Who Sees*.

For the first time in the more than fifty-five years of my crazy career, I put on a hat I'd never worn before: director. Then for four days, we filmed in the extraordinarily majestic, desolate, vibrant, resplendent promised land of my forefathers.

I felt reborn all over again. I was completely aware that every gift and every dream my Creator had placed in me in my mother's womb was finally being birthed. Everything I'd ever discovered and learned during every moment onstage, in front of cameras, microphones, audiences, and critics, was culminating in this experience. It was beyond humbling. It was beyond thrilling.

Have you recently stepped out of your
comfort zone? What did you do? How did
the outcome change your mindset?

What can you do for yourself that will allow you to take
more risks and step outside of your comfort zone?

God's Plan

What might seem weird because we're not used to it ultimately becomes something beautiful that God created with the sole and "soul" purpose to delight us. I marvel at the way God works: He always does something abundantly better than anything we initially imagine.

From the moment I met Claude Kelly and Chuck Harmony, I was a goner. Separately they are responsible for bringing us some of pop music's biggest hits with artists like Michael Jackson, Whitney Houston, Beyoncé, Rihanna, Miley Cyrus, Bruno Mars, and Lady Gaga. You name the superstar and they've either written or produced that star's hits—or both. Along with their industry successes they each were left with an aching emptiness in their souls and a deep longing for purpose in their lives and in their work. Independent of each other they left the music business—Claude to study the world's religions and Chuck to attend seminary. I instantly clicked with Claude and Chuck—they were treasured, trusted little brothers to me.

We agreed to write "Finally," an idea I had originally

written for a future film, way down the road as one of the sequels to *Then Came You*. I initially envisioned it as a love song about a character who, after years of wasted living traveling the world as a musician, finally finds real love. We began writing with that intent.

The God Who Sees had just released, but Claude and Chuck had not yet seen it. We took a break for a lunch and began to watch it.

Not two minutes in they both shouted out various reactions of the same thing: "This is it! This is what we've been searching for! This is why we're here! This is how we're supposed to theatricalize our music!"

We were all excited, and I immediately blurted out, "Guys, this isn't supposed to be a love song about a man and a woman. This is supposed to be the ultimate love song between God and His children. The prodigal son! We're gonna write the next oratorio—*The God of the Other Side*!"

I said this with the utmost conviction because I knew it in my spirit. They did too. We all immediately said yes, then got back to work to finish the song, thrilled by our newfound purpose.

Years ago God told me something I've never forgotten: "There are no crumbs on My table, Kathie. I use *everything* for good for My good purpose." God had a different plan. A better plan than any of us had initially imagined.

Have you ever had a plan that ended up
unfolding in a completely different way? How
did God's plan change everything?

Have you met people who changed your life and became an
integral part of God's plan? Who did you meet? How did
things change? Are those people still a part of your life?

DAY 43

Timing Is Everything

One day I got to tell Al Pacino, "I'm sorry, but you're just going to have to audition."

He had just won the Golden Globe for Best Actor in the television miniseries *Angels in America*.

I had met Al years before through our mutual longtime friend Anna Strasberg, who is the widow of the legendary acting coach Lee Strasberg. Lee developed methods for The Actors Studio, where famed actors like Marilyn Monroe, Paul Newman, and, yes, Al Pacino studied. Al had seen my off-Broadway musical *Under the Bridge* and had instructed his assistant to call me about it.

"Hello, Mrs. Gifford. Mr. Pacino would like you to send him *The People Under the Stairs*."

I laughed. "You mean *The Family Under the Bridge*?"

He laughed too. "Yes, please."

"Okay," I responded. "Does he want the screenplay or the stage version?"

"Both," he said, hedging his bets.

When we met in California to discuss the project he casually mentioned, "You know I've done some pretty good work in my life."

No kidding, I thought.

"But nothing my children can see." (His twins were very young at the time.) "And I love this script."

He then went on for about half an hour, digging into technical actor stuff about the character arc for Armand (the lead), the dynamic with the children, the antagonist . . . you get the picture.

I finally had to politely interrupt him because he had never mentioned the music, which I had cowritten with my friend David Pomeranz.

"Al, I'm sorry, but you *do* know this is a musical, right?"

He immediately looked at Anna and declared, "Why doesn't anyone think I can sing? I started my career in musical theater!"

I thought he'd just chuckle at that, but no, Al immediately

stood up, pushed himself away from the table, and began to sing "The Star-Spangled Banner," in full throat and totally in tune.

Everyone was stunned. Finally, I leaned over to him and said, "All right! You've got the job!"

It's one of my favorite moments to remember. After that, every time I'd see Al he'd say, "When are we going to make my movie?" God knows I'd been trying everything in my arsenal to get it made, but the timing was always off. Such is Hollywood. Some things happen overnight, others take more to come to fruition, and most never get done at all.

Do you have a project that you've always wanted to complete but the timing is always off? What is it?

How do you personally stay motivated to create when you have other projects or goals on hold?

Power Outage

*Y*ears ago I got a request from a wonderful friend of mine, Pastor Ray, to join him on a TV special he was going to tape at the California Men's Colony in San Luis Obispo, California. This was a maximum-security prison at the time and held a few thousand inmates.

"Pat Boone's going to be there too," Pastor Ray said. "Can you and Michie come as well?"

My sister, Michie, and I had joined Pastor Ray in his prison ministry several times before, and we had always been honored to be a part of his beautiful and Christlike outpouring of love to these broken men behind bars. So, naturally, I said we'd love to be a part of his television special.

A few weeks later Michie arrived ahead of me in San Luis Obispo.

"Okay, there's good news and bad news," she told me over the phone. "The good news is I just survived the worst turbulence in my life but landed safely here."

"Okay, good," I said. "What's the bad news?"

"The bad news is I just arrived at the prison and Tex Watson is my bodyguard."

"What!" I screamed. "Tex Watson, the man who actually butchered the victims in the Manson murders?"

"Yes," Michie responded. "But, Kath, he's asked Jesus into his life, and I swear, he's a changed, redeemed man. His eyes are clear and beautiful and full of light. You're going to love him."

Love him? I was incredulous. Yet when I arrived I discovered that everything she had told me was true. Charles "Tex" Watson was a transformed creation in Christ, completely delivered from the drugs and the demons and the unspeakable violence of his former life under Charles Manson's influence. One look into his eyes convinced me of that.

It was 114 degrees outside when Michie and I arrived at the prison. We had been instructed to wear clothing that completely covered our bodies, from our necks to our wrists to our ankles, with no revealing flesh. No makeup, no jewelry. Nothing that could be considered at all alluring.

Before long, we were assembled on the stage in front of thousands of California inmates.

Pat Boone sang, Michie and I sang, Pastor Ray preached, and Tex shared his life-transforming testimony. The warden and his wife sat in the front row, and all was going well until suddenly the power went out and we were left stranded and vulnerable, struggling to adjust to the darkness in the already stifling amphitheater.

The terrifying reality of our situation quickly became apparent as prison guards rushed to remove the warden and his wife to safety, leaving Pastor Ray, Pat Boone, Tex Watson, and my sister and me alone on a dim stage. We held hands and sang "What a Friend We Have in Jesus" while thousands of hard-core inmates, many bare chested in the heat, yelled out "Sing 'Helter Skelter'" and masturbated.

My life passed before me in the ensuing moments. I am ashamed to admit that I actually thought to myself, *I don't want to die looking like this.*

Suddenly the power came on and the guards were able to move all of us from the stage to safety.

I'll never forget that day. Do you have an epic true story that stops people in their tracks? What happened?

Wild things happen to all of us. Is there a particular thing that happened and changed your mindset or impacted how you go about your daily life?

DAY 45
Saying Goodbye to Home

*O*ur 1920s Mediterranean home on Long Island Sound has been my favorite place in the world ever since we bought it and moved in on Cassidy's first birthday, August 2, 1994. Frank and I knew it was a miracle that we were able to purchase it. The house already had one offer on it from a wealthy Wall Street guy for way more than we could afford. But we made the best offer we could and started praying— barely breathing for four days while our realtor tried to seal the deal.

Finally, he called with the incredible news that the owner had agreed to sell the house to us.

"What? How did we get it? That's impossible!" we responded incredulously. "We offered way less."

The realtor told us, "I know. I'm telling you, in all my years in real estate I've never seen or heard anything like this."

It seems that years ago the owner had attended a pro-am tennis event for charity. He paid a lot of money to play tennis with an elite group of athletes. But when he arrived and went to sign in, he discovered that his name was nowhere on the list of attendees. He was upset and embarrassed until suddenly someone came up next to him, put his hand out to shake, and said, "Hi, I'm Frank Gifford. How would you like to play with me today?"

The realtor chuckled. "He was a huge Giants fan and now he was face-to-face with his favorite player of all time." All these years later, when it was time to decide whose offer to accept, he said, "I want Frank Gifford to own my house."

There was never a moment in all the ensuing years that Frank and I didn't marvel at the miracle. We kept expecting the real owners to show up at any moment and kick us out.

As the years passed, life brought many changes. Our kids moved to Southern California to pursue their dreams. Frank passed away in our sunroom, and my precious mother, Joanie, died two years later. Our home was a sanctuary for many decades and provided so much abundance. But with everyone now gone except for me this once magnificent, bustling, filled-to-the-rafters-with-music-and-laughter home became a large, looming reminder of all that I had lost in my life. We'd had a daily tradition of toasting the sunset every evening and I realized that I couldn't do it anymore.

Maya Angelou said, "I long, as does every human being, to be at home wherever I find myself." I had so many precious memories of living on Old Greenwich Harbor, but it was no longer home, so I decided to venture on and find my new home.

Have you ever moved away from home?
How did the change make you feel? Did
it turn out to be a positive move?

Sometimes a place is meant for a specific
season and venturing away from it can cause
you to feel uncomfortable. Can you think of
a place that served you well for a season?

DAY 46

Listen and Trust

I've always had a keen sense of finality about certain things. I've come to understand it's a moving of the Holy Spirit—a voice I've learned to listen to and trust.

I went through the motions for the next few years—getting up early, climbing in the car for the commute to New York, and smiling and laughing for our wonderful viewers one *TODAY* after another. No one but my family and my closest friends knew the depth of the depression I was battling. I cried out to God for an answer, and as always, He spoke to my heart from His Word. "I know the plans I have for you . . . plans to prosper you and not to harm you, plans to give you hope and a future" (Jer. 29:11).

Two years prior, in 2017, I had given notice to my bosses at NBC that I would be leaving the show to finally follow my childhood dreams of movies and music. While they understood, they pleaded with me to stay and help them navigate the turbulent circumstances we were going through with the various personnel upheavals (Matt Lauer, Billy Bush, Megyn Kelly, to name a few) being played out on a daily basis in the media. It's not easy to report the news when you're actually making the news you're supposed to report.

I continued to stay until I just couldn't stay any longer. The Holy Spirit told me it was time to move on and I needed to listen.

On April 5, 2019, after eleven amazing years with my now dear friend Hoda, I said goodbye to *TODAY* and hello to tomorrow.

I've learned that it is important to challenge yourself and be willing to get out of your comfort zone because that is the only way you will continue to grow.

Has the Holy Spirit ever spoken to you? What did the Holy Spirit say? How did you respond?

Can you think of a time you stepped out of your comfort zone and took a leap of faith? What did you do? What was the outcome? How has it affected your future?

DAY 47

My Future

*S*o many people ask me if I think I'll ever get married again. "I have no idea," I always answer. "I don't know what my future holds, but I know the One who holds my future."

I don't mean it to sound like some pat cliché. I say it because I know it's true. I've been blessed with a great love, and only God knows if Frank was my last one. Honestly, I hope not. I have such a full, vibrant, and exciting life. I'd love nothing more than to share it with someone who understands it, values it, and enjoys it as much as I do.

That's an intimidating thing to many men. They're not used to strong, independent women who know what they want and refuse to settle for less than what God desires for them. Men have tried to control history for so long that they're resistant to sharing the reins. But I'm okay with that. Any man who's afraid *of* me is not the man *for* me.

I love Proverbs 31, which says of the godly woman: "She laughs at the future" (v. 25 LEB).

That's where I find myself now—feeling decades younger than I obviously am. "Fired up," as my friend George Shinn calls it, with God's endless promises and possibilities.

Psalm 5:3 says, "In the morning, LORD, you hear my voice; in the morning I lay my requests before you and wait expectantly." I smile when I read that every morning. I actually transpose it just a bit to read "wait and *expect* and *see*!"

I believe in an all-loving, all-seeing, all-good, gift-giving God. My oratorios are all about His character—His shalom: faithfulness, loving-kindness, justice, benevolence, joyfulness, peacefulness, and righteousness. He sees me. He sees you. And the greatest miracle? He loves us anyway.

The greatest way to make the most outrageous, transformational change in your life at *any time* of your life is right here, right now. *Believe Him.*

Have you been blessed with a great love? Who? What are some of your favorite memories you've spent together?

Has love made outrageous, transformational changes in your life? How?

Other People's Opinions Aren't Your Business

I received so much criticism from Christians early in my career, basically asking me, "How can you call yourself a Christian and be in show business?"

To which I always replied, "How can I be in show business and *not* be a Christian?" There is simply no way I could have survived the constant rejection and brutality—both psychological and physical at times—that are part and parcel with show business. I knew God had called me to this business. He knew His plans for me in my mother's womb. He saw me being formed. And He saw all the millions of people who would eventually hear about Jesus because He placed a boldness in me to proclaim His truth to the masses.

No one has the right to judge another person. Besides, the same judgment we declare over others will be declared over we who do the judging (Matt. 7:1–2). We need to remind ourselves every day that "all have sinned and fallen short of the glory of God" (Rom. 3:23).

All means all—you and me and everyone else on the planet. God desires that we love one another and leave the judging to the only One who ever lived a perfect life, which He willingly gave up that we might have life and life abundantly (John 10:10).

After all, "We love Him because He loved us first" (1 John 4:19 RGT).

I've learned to not put a lot of stock into what other people think or vocalize as their opinion. It simply doesn't matter because I am a child of God. He didn't create us to judge each other and proclaim the truths that only He can proclaim. We shouldn't allow others to influence our lives and cause us to stray away from the abundant life our glorious God created for us.

Have you experienced judgment or targeted rejection from other people? How did you handle it?

Think about the peace you have once you've followed God's plans and allowed him to unfold life's abundance. How did your life change? What worries were you able to let go of?

God Loves You

*P*eople ask me all the time if I had any knowledge of Bruce Jenner's decision about his gender during that time. No, I didn't. Bruce and Frank were very close. There were very few men that Frank considered his peers, but Bruce was one of them. Frank wasn't arrogant about his fame and his accomplishments, but very few men had ever achieved his level of success in one of the most difficult arenas in the world—sports.

Bruce was affable and fun. He was also dyslexic. Frank could relate because, as a young man, he had stuttered. So, Frank mentored Bruce in the television world, just as he mentored me. He taught him about the ins and outs of professional sportscasting, and he took great pride as he watched Bruce navigate the treacherous new waters of being in front of the camera.

Frank was as stunned and taken by surprise as the rest of the world when Bruce identified as a woman and announced that he wanted to change his gender.

By that time Bruce and Kris had divorced and were living separate lives. Several days before the infamous interview with Diane Sawyer was scheduled to air, Bruce called me. I was happy to hear his familiar, distinctive voice.

"Kathie," he said after we exchanged pleasantries, "do you hate me?"

"Hate you?" I exclaimed, "Of course not, Bruce. I could never hate you. I love you."

"But your faith . . ." he started.

I prayed silently that God would give me the grace to speak words of hope and life to my sweet friend.

"Bruce, God created you. You may believe He made a mistake with you, but God doesn't make mistakes. We do."

He was silent on the other end of the line.

"Sweetie, He knows you. He sees you. He loves you." My heart beat heavily in my chest.

"Whatever you do to your body—whatever changes you make—you can never change the masterpiece you are that He created. He created you in His image. And when you die, as we all will, that body will decay. Ashes to ashes, dust to dust. But the eternal part of you—your soul—will go on forever. And He will make you perfect. That is the hope of eternal life in Him."

I could sense him taking this in, processing the enormity and wonder and miracle of it.

"Thank you, Kath," he simply said.

"Are you going to change your name?" I asked. By now my heart was broken because his was.

"Yes," he said, "to Caitlyn."

"It's a beautiful name," I said. And it is. "I love you, Caitlyn."

She called me just once again, soon after. And we tried to get together in New York City, but our schedules were crazy because life is crazy. It changes every nanosecond. But God doesn't. He is the same yesterday, today, and forever. He loves us. His heart breaks for us. But He never gives up on us. Never miss an opportunity to tell your friends that God loves them.

Have you had to remind a friend that God
loved them? What was their reaction?

How can you show your friends and family on a
regular basis that God loves them? How do you need
to change the way you live to accomplish this?

Unfailing Love

*W*e don't know how much time we will get to live. In a blink of an eye, everything can change. I have been criticized for years for my continued association with the Kardashian family, but I couldn't care less what people think. Kris Jenner and I have been friends since the late 1970s. Frank and I were asked to be godparents to Kendall and Kylie and we joyfully agreed.

When they were little, I sent my two goddaughters a darling Amish-made playhouse. It was just like the one I had purchased for Cassidy at our house. I included all the precious furniture and accessories for it, hoping it would bring the girls the same pleasure it had brought to Cass. They loved it.

While visiting the family years later, I attended a launch party for Kylie's new line of children's products named after her daughter, Stormi. Kris got up and said, "Come here, Kathie. I want to show you something in the backyard."

I dutifully followed her into Kylie's immaculate, fairy-filled backyard. Kris led me to a delightful little house nestled among the trees.

"Remember, Kath?" she said with a smile. "This is the playhouse you had made for Kendall and Kylie when they were little girls. I had it refurbished when Stormi was born."

I was stunned. It was beyond beautiful.

"But look," she continued, opening the little door, "I kept all the original furniture and the little stove and the little refrigerator and all the dishes, pots, and pans."

I could hear our Savior speaking to me, drawing on the wisdom in Isaiah 43:19: "Behold, I make all things new, Kathie! Do you not perceive it?"

A few moments later Kylie found me. She was holding a tiny charm bracelet.

"You gave me this, right?" she asked as I focused on the little Tiffany treasure. "I'm saving it now for Stormi."

To which Kendall—all five-feet-ten-perfect-model inches of her added, "And I look at the picture of you and me every morning next to my sink in my bathroom."

On that day, Kobe Bryant and his thirteen-year-old daughter perished in a helicopter crash. Kobe and Vanessa and their four beautiful children were good friends of the Kardashian/Jenner family. They'd recently spent New Year's Eve together. Everyone tried, in their own way, to make sense of the senseless. We prayed for Vanessa and her now three children. We prayed for the other families who lost loved ones as the details of the crash began to emerge.

As I sat in the car on my way back to my hotel, I marveled once again at the faithfulness of God and His unfailing love. We must appreciate the time we've shared with our loved ones and the unfailing love that God has bestowed upon us.

Do you have friends who've become family?
Who are these friends? What are your most
cherished memories you've shared with them?

Have you experienced a loss that put things into
perspective and inspired you to make shifts within
your life? What changes did you make?

DAY 51

Lifelong Friendship

I cherish Regis's friendship. I cherish the memories, and I cherish all the moments we shared when we had the privilege of making America laugh. When I was presented with the Moving Visionary Award in January 2020 it was given to me by best friend Regis.

Before accepting the award, I whispered a prayer. "Lord, give me the words to say. Please, Lord, I have no idea why I'm here or what Your purpose is. Just speak through me."

I have *never* written a speech. I have always just asked God to lead me, and He always has. Always. So, I waited nervously for Reege to take the stage. Finally, he did, and to much love and applause from the audience. I was happy to hear the reaction of yet another audience that has enjoyed and appreciated him for so long. But then he began to struggle with the teleprompter. He got a little confused, and I could sense the audience's concern for him too. Finally, he said, "And in my forty-five years in this business I spent fifteen of them with Kathie Lee, and they were the best fifteen years in my whole career."

I smiled.

"So, let's bring her onstage right now to accept the Visionary Award—Kathie Lee . . . *Griffin*!"

The audience gasped.

I was thrilled and threw myself to my feet, seizing the golden opportunity.

"It's *Gifford*," I yelled at him. Regis looked for the voice.

"It is?" he asked, and the audience roared. "Are you sure?"

The audience went wild. It was the only unscripted, genuinely funny moment of the very long evening. As I approached the stage to accept the award, I thanked the Lord for bringing us back to the classic *Live with Regis and Kathie Lee* days. It was a gift.

A lovely young lady handed me the award, and with joy, I hugged this dear friend of mine. "You're killing me," I whispered in his ear, then turned to the audience and said, "And you think you know somebody!"

I've been incredibly blessed to have several truly best friends—Regis is a prime example.

Do you have a best friend who makes everything better? Who is that person? How have they impacted your life?

When was the last time you reached out to your best friend and reminded them how special they are?

DAY 52

Friends Who Make Us Better

A real friend makes you feel better about yourself. Friends help you cope when you think you're done and offer hope that it can get better. They love you as you are but won't let you stay that way. Clearly, having friends improves our lives.

Hoda Kotb is a best friend that I'm so blessed to have. I miss sitting next to her every day. I have watched her evolve from an award-winning journalist, *Dateline* Hoda, into an extraordinarily natural and captivating television presence, Happy Hour Hoda.

She anchored with Savannah Guthrie in isolation due to COVID-19. I watched her break down during this difficult time on the show. Hoda was interviewing one of her favorite people from one of her favorite cities—Drew Brees from New Orleans—as he announced his extraordinary gift of $5 million to battle the pandemic in their beloved city.

"Something else is contagious too," Hoda told him, "generosity."

And then she simply began to give in to the raw emotion and frazzled nerves and sheer exhaustion of showing up for weeks trying to do her job with her usual grace, professionalism, and passion. I think it was the defining moment of her extraordinary career.

I wept with her. That's her gift. She shows up authentic and optimistic and then she smiles that Hoda smile and laughs that Hoda laugh, and sometimes—in rare, unpredictable moments—she cries those Hoda tears.

That's why I love her. That's why everybody loves her. I stayed at *TODAY* ten years longer than I had planned because I fell in love with her. She was awarded yet another

Emmy for her rock-solid coverage of this pandemic, but all she cares about is rushing home to her precious children and creating another memory.

I celebrate her. I admire her. I love her to pieces. And I lift up my glass as we did countless times and say, "Brava, Hoda Mama! You're the best."

Do you have a friend who has a gift and makes everything brighter? Who? How did you meet them?

Vulnerability is a superpower. How has being vulnerable with your friends made your bond closer?

DAY 53

Purpose

*I*f I wake up every morning and I still have a pulse, that means I still have a purpose too. Paul Newman taught me that years ago.

It was a bitterly cold Sunday night, and I had left Frank

sitting by a blazing fire watching football. I had promised many weeks earlier to attend a fundraiser for the Westport Country Playhouse at a home two coves over from ours.

I remember driving there on the icy road and thinking, *Why did I say yes to this?*

Soon after I arrived I heard a commotion near the front door. I turned around to see who was causing it. Paul Newman, who always sent both women and men into a frenzy, had just walked in. I didn't want to be yet another pushy person vying for his attention, so I moved into the next room, hoping I'd get a chance to say hello later in the evening.

I felt a tap on my back. I turned around and there was Paul. He immediately got down on one knee, took both of my hands in both of his, kissed them, and said, "Hi, Kathie. How are you?"

It was surreal. I said, "Oh, Paul, it's so good to see you! It's been too long. How are you?"

He struggled a little to get up and said, "Honey, I'm eighty years old but I've still got a pulse. And that's a good thing."

I remember going home and telling Frank the story and how moved I was that Paul was still using his celebrity to make the world a better place—even a dilapidated old theater in Connecticut.

Frank didn't buy it. "You just love his eyes," he said with a laugh.

As I went to bed that night, I knew Paul had taught me something that I'd take with me for the rest of my life: if I have a pulse, I have a purpose. And you do too.

How has your purpose changed someone else's circumstance? Has your purpose allowed you to save someone from the edge?

How has your purpose evolved throughout your life?

No Regrets

There are so many more stories I wish I could tell you: some crazy, some heartwarming, some heartbreaking, and many just too incredible to be true. But I can't because the people involved matter to me, and they've asked me not to share them. They needn't worry. Their secrets are safe with me. And I pray to God that my secrets are safe with them. It's never too late to keep a secret and save a friend, right?

None of us knows when we will breathe our last breath. Frank didn't, my parents didn't, and I won't either. But I know where I'm going, and I know who is waiting for me there. I have great peace in my soul from walking with my Savior since I was twelve years old, discovering through every day of every decade that *God is faithful in all things and in all ways*.

I pray that on the day I die I will have learned something brand-new or will have done something I've never done before or written the best lyric He's ever given me.

Because it's never too late until, yes, one day it actually is.

I want to know that I have lived a joyful life. Joy is non-negotiable. You've got to fight for joy in life. You've got to battle for it. Certain things are negotiable in life. But, joy, if you don't have joy in your life, what do you have?

Life really is too short, and I want to live each day knowing that I lived the abundant life that God wrote for me. Make the decision for yourself, right now. Agree to never waste a moment. Never allow yourself to be too fearful to try something new. Always love your people and stand by them. Be vulnerable and say the things on your heart.

Is there something you've been wanting
to learn or try? Make plans to do that
thing so you won't have any regrets.

Is there something you've been wanting to share
with someone? Set up a meeting or pick up
the phone. Don't leave anything unsaid.

DAY 55

Check In with Yourself

I think it is important to check in with yourself on a regular
basis. Sometimes we lose sight of who we truly are and our
purpose. Having an honest conversation with yourself allows
you to assess your mistakes and determine what adjust-
ments you need to make. You'll have an opportunity to be
humbled and identify what you need to change. Moreover,
you'll show up more authentically and intentionally for the
people most dear to you.

A check-in looks different for everyone. Mine looks
something like this:

I have only been in love three times in my life. I've been
married twice, dated many men, and made too many bad
choices through the years, in both my personal and my professional lives.

I've walked the walk of shame. I've been sexually harassed, sexually abused, and date-raped.

I have tried to live a life of integrity, and more times than I want to admit, I have failed miserably.

I've smiled many phony smiles when I was aching to cry real tears.

I've railed at God privately while publicly praising Him.

I have cared way too often what other people thought of me and thought way too much of myself way too many times.

I have tried to please people who don't matter instead of pleasing my Creator, the only One who does.

I have achieved great heights, and I have hit rock bottom.

I have been lied about, and I have lied too.

I have lived with great sorrow and profound poverty of my soul.

I have sinned.

But I have been forgiven.

I am a child of God.

Recite your own self check-in. Did you
learn anything about yourself?

What changes would you like to make so you can move
forward in a more fulfilling, purpose-driven way?

Never Give Up

In 1975 I moved to Los Angeles to give myself one year to make it into a brutal Hollywood business. I survived shooting commercials, acting as an extra, and singing in Vegas. At times it was fleeting but I continued to work hard and hold onto my dream.

After I was rejected for a children's show audition, my agent called me to say, "Kath, they want to see you for a new game show over at Ralph Edwards Productions. Have three songs ready."

"Okay," I agreed, wearily. *Here we go again.*

When I arrived at the audition, I thought someone had made a mistake. There was no one else waiting with me.

"Kathie Epstein?" she said.

"Yes," I answered. "Where is everybody?"

"It's just you," she replied. "Mr. Edwards will see you now."

I followed her into a large conference room full of people I'd never seen before. Except for one: the head writer of the children's show that I'd thought for sure I was going to get a month before. His name was Gary Bloom, and he smiled a big smile and winked at me.

What is going on? I wondered.

All I could do was launch into the songs I'd prepared. I had barely finished the last one when the legendary producer Ralph Edwards walked over to me to shake my hand.

"Welcome to Ralph Edwards Productions." He smiled graciously. "Welcome to *Name That Tune*."

I was stunned. In an instant, my entire life changed. The trajectory of my career went through the roof and nothing would ever be the same.

As it turned out, Gary Bloom had told my agent that while he had loved my earlier audition, he thought I was too sophisticated for the children's show. But he was working on another show that he was sure I'd be perfect for.

He was right. I learned two hundred songs in five days and shot the shows for the entire year in a few weeks.

We taped at NBC Studios in Burbank right next to *The Tonight Show*, and, finally, I thought, *So this is what it's like to make a living doing what you love to do.*

As I walked through the gate for the first time with my agent and parents, past the security guard who greeted me warmly, I whispered this prayer: "Dear Jesus, I know my life is about to change. Thank You, Lord, for this amazing new chapter in my life. Please help me to treat every single person I meet exactly the same—from the executive producers to the guard at the gate. And I will give You all the praise."

I squeezed my daddy's hand. He was still smiling because the guard had confused him with one of his all-time heroes, Roy Rogers.

"Hi, Roy," he had said to him. "Welcome back."

"Thank you, kindly," my daddy had responded, never letting on.

We giggled.

A few weeks later we wrapped the season, and I headed to the car in the parking lot feeling elated. It had gone well. I hadn't made one mistake in two hundred songs. I was on my way. My daddy came up after me, and the same security guard stopped him.

"Mr. Epstein," he said, "I just want you to know that every time your daughter came through the gate, love came with her."

"Thank you kindly," my daddy answered with tears in his eyes.

Hard work always pays off. Have you experienced a similar situation where your dreams and goals felt unattainable?

The way you treat people speaks volumes about who you are as a human being.

※ ※ ※

Did you accomplish a goal that required extra effort and perseverance? What was it? How long did it take you to accomplish it, and what hurdles did you face?

People will never forget how you made them feel. What do you do to make feel people seen and loved?

Sweet Memories

I have always been fascinated to hear the stories of how people first met. A moment that seems insignificant sometimes turns into a momentous shift in one's destiny.

Frank Gifford was my husband for almost twenty-nine years. None of my memories of him have faded. I can even still smell him. I know I always will.

I don't actually recall our very first face-to-face meeting, but obviously when I did meet him I discovered that his face rivaled his gluteus maximus. Even at fifty-two years old he was matinee-idol handsome. And sweet and modest. We liked each other instantly, but I was twenty-nine and getting divorced and he was on his second marriage with three children and a grandchild.

We began a beautiful friendship that deepened through the next four years as Frank experienced loss and tragedy and heartbreak in his personal life. Anytime he was facing a difficult situation he called me to see if he could take me to lunch or dinner. I felt privileged that he would seek my comfort and company.

I had started dating someone in 1984 who Frank didn't like at all for me. He didn't like the way this boyfriend treated me and kept asking why I stayed in such a roller-coaster relationship with a man who obviously didn't love me.

I was in a terrible romantic rut. The kind where one day you're euphoric and the next you're miserable. But I couldn't seem to find the strength to get out. Frank was determined to be the strength I needed, and he kept his word. His marriage to his second wife had deteriorated and was in the final stages of divorce. He was faithful to continue to be my friend and accompany me to whatever was going on in my life—whether it was personal or professional.

Frank asked me to marry him on August 10, 1986. On Saturday, October 18, I became his wife in a small, quiet ceremony on the beach.

It's always so sweet to remember back to how we met, became friends, and then joined together as man and wife.

Think of someone special in your life. A best friend, a partner, or maybe a mentor. How did you meet?

What is one of your most cherished memories that you shared with that special person?

Power of Prayer

I had had an amazing fifteen-year run with Regis, and an equally amazing but different eleven-year run with Hoda. But the five days I spent hosting with Craig Ferguson while Hoda was on maternity leave were mind-blowing. The constant energy, the unpredictability, the side-splitting hysteria were all things I'd never experienced.

Before Craig left to go home, we agreed that we wanted to write a movie together. At two o'clock the next morning I woke up knowing just what our movie should be. I started writing and didn't stop until noon when I called Craig—of course he was shocked.

I sent him the script and he called me the next day. "Kathie, this is your baby. I stand ready to serve."

I think my scream of joy must have been heard in the Highlands. The ensuing months were a blur. Writing, rewriting, calling investors, rewriting again, flying to Nashville to write the songs, recording the songs, shooting the videos of the songs . . . all of it. There was only one snag—we were scheduled to shoot in June, and we had *not one penny* invested by February. I needed $5.7 million or it wasn't going to happen. Movies are incredibly risky crapshoots. Only fools or insanely wealthy people tend to be willing to invest in them.

With a deadline fast approaching, we needed a miracle. My friends and I prayed. A friend, Anne Ferrell Tata, cried out, "George Shinn." We called him and he looped in his money man, Spencer. The rest is a miracle.

The next day, and against all odds and anything that makes sense in a real world, George Shinn agreed to executive produce a movie he had never read by a woman he had never met to be shot in four months in a place he'd never been to.

This story is God's truth and proof of the power of prayer. You should always trust God to provide everything you need. And though you may not have written a movie or be needing to finance it, I'm sure there are things you've gone after that could be identified as "more than you can chew." If so, consider this your nudge to do what I did—stop, drop, and pray.

✿ ✿ ✿

What should you be praying about
that you haven't prayed for?

Can you think of a specific experience or season
where the power of prayer shined? What were
you praying about? How did God provide?

Music for the Soul

If you've never heard Charles "Wigg" Walker sing, you've never heard the best soul singer. My friend Tom owns the Acme Feed and Seed where Wigg performs.

I had never heard of Wigg, but Tom assured me he was legendary in the Nashville music industry. Jimi Hendrix had been his guitarist. James Brown had kicked him off his tour bus because Wigg was pulling even better audience response than Brown.

"Nashville didn't become famous at first for country music, Kathie. It was black music first."

Cody and his wife, Erika, and Cass and her husband, Ben, joined me, Angie, and Greg and we headed downtown.

Wigg was already singing when we arrived. I simply could not believe the sound that was coming from this thin, frail, seventy-nine-year-old man. It was the purest, most thrilling voice you can imagine. Powerful beyond description. And seemingly effortless. I was mesmerized. I couldn't sit still. I had to get up and groove to the music he was making. Wigg noticed and very sweetly said hello from the stage.

Suddenly Tom said, "Go up there and sing with him, Kathie."

"What? No way!" I told him.

But Tom insisted, and Tom is used to charming everyone to do what he wants. So, I went onstage.

I can't describe what singing with Wigg was like except that he made me fearless. Brett James had bamboozled me to sing again a couple years before, but Wigg made me sing notes I've never hit before. With no rehearsal, no warm-up, no finding the right key, I simply joined him on his journey. It was musical magic for me from the very first note.

Wigg was happy, too, and so it began that each time I came to hear him at Acme I'd join him onstage for a few songs.

That man brings out the inner Aretha in me I didn't even know existed. I'm fearless with him. I don't give a rip, I let it fly, and it's so fun. Wigg represents to me all that was just fun, and good and real about an authentic person who gets up on that stage and sings their brains out the way God made them to do.

Is there an authentic person in your life who brings out the best in everyone? Who?

Music has healing powers. Is there a particular artist or genre of music that brings life to your soul? Has music helped you find joy?

Final Goodbyes

*T*hose of us who knew Regis best and spent time with him in the last two years of his life could sadly see the inevitable coming. It was the same with Frank, and my mother and father. They began disappearing little by little. They changed in small ways, and then the changes began to accelerate. Finally, they began sleeping more, eating less, and losing interest in the things they once loved. It's heartbreaking when it happens, but it does help you prepare emotionally for your final goodbye.

Regis could walk into a United Nations gathering filled with people from all over the world who spoke thirty different languages and have them all in stitches within thirty seconds. He never had an enemy because he never made one. He was kind to everyone, took notice of everyone, and if he really liked someone, he would tease them mercilessly. Yes, that was the ultimate Regis Philbin "seal of approval" compliment.

I was entirely charmed by him for thirty-five years, along with the rest of the world. But there were many, many private times with him as well that were much more serious in nature. I cherish the memories of those as well.

The last time I saw Reege was in June 2020. I invited

Regis and Joy to come to my house for lunch. When Regis got out on the passenger side of their car, I immediately saw that he was much more frail than he'd been some six months prior when I saw him in LA. We sat in my screened porch and enjoyed a delicious lunch of his favorite, *frutti di mare*, and laughed as we had for almost four decades.

After several hours they hugged me goodbye and got into their car to drive home.

I was happy/sad, you know? So happy to see my precious friend again, but so sad to admit that it might have been for the last time.

A few weeks later, back in Tennessee, I felt the Lord telling me to get on the next plane in the morning and go home. I had no idea why, but I have learned through the years not to ignore His promptings. I had no sooner walked into my door in Connecticut when my friend Angie texted me, "I'm so sorry about Regis ☹."

"What?" I texted back, and she told me the news that Regis had passed. I was stunned but not surprised. I actually rejoiced, just as I had when I had held Frank in my arms just moments after his passing, almost five years earlier.

And just like Frank, Regis was with Jesus. He was truly home.

The next day I drove over to see Joy and her beautiful daughters, Joanna and J. J. I didn't stay long. As Joy walked me to the door, she told me something I will never forget for the rest of my days.

"He hadn't laughed for a long time, Kathie, and I was truly getting worried about him. But then we came to your house for lunch, and you both just picked up right where you left off the time before."

I nodded, remembering, tearing up.

"That was the last time I heard Regis laugh."

Have you said goodbye to a loved one with the thought that it might be your last goodbye? Were you emotionally prepared?

What is one memory of that person
you'll always cherish the most?

Notes

1. Lawrence K. Altman, "Deaths from AIDs Decline Sharply in New York City," *New York Times*, January 25, 1997, https://www.nytimes.com/1997/01/25/nyregion/deaths-from-aids-decline-sharply-in-new-york-city.html.
2. Michael M. Homan, "Did the Ancient Israelites Drink Beer?," *Biblical Archaeology Review* 35, no. 5 (September/October 2010), https://www.baslibrary.org/biblical-archaeology-review/36/5/4.
3. 1 Corinthians 13:4–8 ESV.
4. Billy Graham, Congressional Gold Medal acceptance speech, United States Capitol, May 2, 1996, Washington, DC, C-Span video, 53:09, https://www.c-span.org/video/?71572-1/congressional-gold-medal.